COMPLETE BOOK OF
Grade

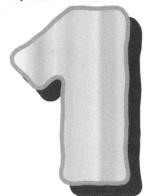

AMERICAN EDUCATION PUBLISHING™

An imprint of Carson-Dellosa Publishing LLC
Greensboro, North Carolina

American Education Publishing™
An imprint of Carson-Dellosa Publishing LLC
P.O. Box 35665
Greensboro, NC 27425 USA

09-074147897

Dear Parents, Caregivers, and Educators,

The *Complete Book* series provides young learners an exciting and dynamic way to learn the basic skills essential to learning success. This vivid workbook will guide your student step-by-step through a variety of engaging and developmentally appropriate activities in basic concepts, reading, math, language arts, writing, and fine motor skills.

The *Complete Book of Grade 1* is designed to be used with an adult's support. Your student will gain the most when you work together through the activities. Below are a few suggestions to help make the most of your learning time together:

- Read the directions aloud. Move your finger under the words as your child watches. As you come to words he or she recognizes, encourage your student to read along.
- Explain the activities in terms your student understands. Talk about the pictures and activities. These conversations will both strengthen your student's confidence and build important language skills.
- Provide support and encouragement to your student. Work with your student at a pace that is comfortable for him or her. End your learning time when your student shows signs of tiring.

To find other learning materials that will interest your young learner and encourage school success, visit www.carsondellosa.com

4

Table of Contents

Reading

About Me

This book belongs to

AidEN

I live at

TDavids

The city I live in is

The state I live in is

My phone number is

Alphabet Action

Directions: Practice writing the letters.

Alphabet Action

Jj

Kk

Ll

Mm

Nn

Oo

Pp

Qq

Rr

Alphabet Action

Ss

Tt

Uu

Vv

Ww

Xx

Yy

Zz

Letter to Letter

Directions: In each set, match the lowercase letter to the uppercase letter.

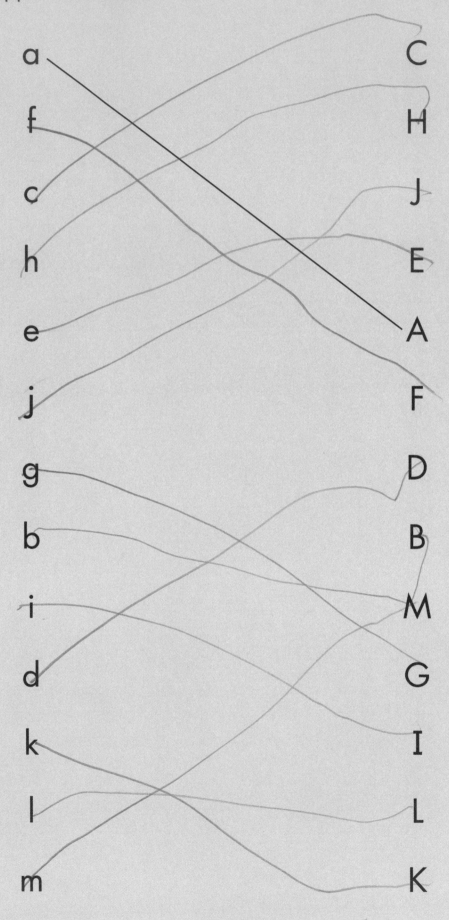

a	C
f	H
c	J
h	E
e	A
j	F
g	D
b	B
i	M
d	G
k	I
l	L
m	K

Letter to Letter

Directions: In each set, match the lowercase letter to the uppercase letter.

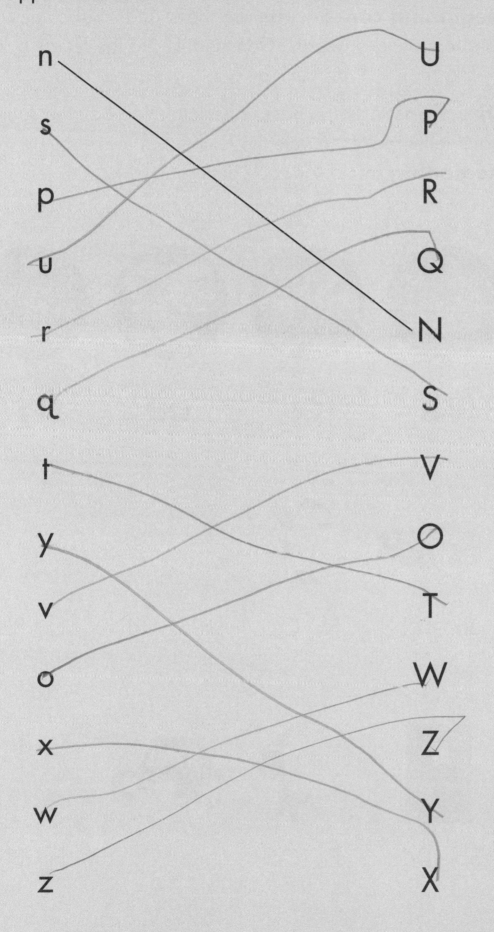

n   U

s   P

p   R

u   Q

r   N

q   S

t   V

y   O

v   T

o   W

x   Z

w   Y

z   X

Consonant Roundup:
B, C, D, F

Beginning consonants are the sounds that come at the beginning of words. Consonants are the letters b, c, d, f, g, h, j, k, l, m, n, p, q, r, s, t, v, w, x, y and z.

Directions: Say the name of each letter. Say the sound each letter makes. Circle the letters that make the **beginning** sound for each picture.

Bb   **Cc**   **Dd**   **Ff**

Bb Dd   Ff Cc   Cc Dd   Ff Bb

Bb Dd   Ff Cc   Cc Dd   Ff Bb

Consonant Roundup:
G, H, J, K

Directions: Say the name of each letter. Say the sound each letter makes. Draw a line from each letter pair to the picture that begins with that sound.

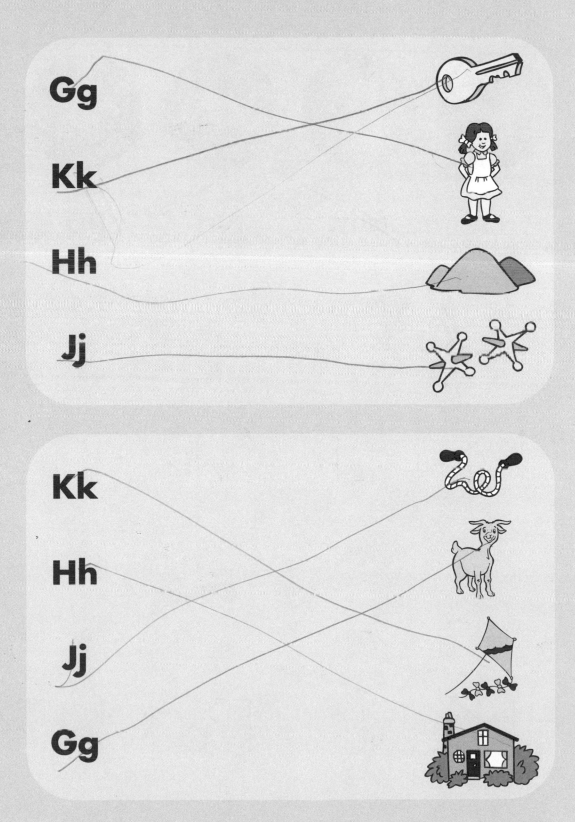

Gg

Kk

Hh

Jj

Kk

Hh

Jj

Gg

Consonant Roundup:
L, M, N, P

Directions: Say the name of each letter. Say the sound each letter makes. Trace the letter pair that makes the beginning sound in each picture.

Ll   **Mm**   **Nn**   **Pp**

Consonant Roundup:
Q, R, S, T

Directions: Say the name of each letter. Say the sound each letter makes. Draw a line from each letter pair to the picture that begins with that sound.

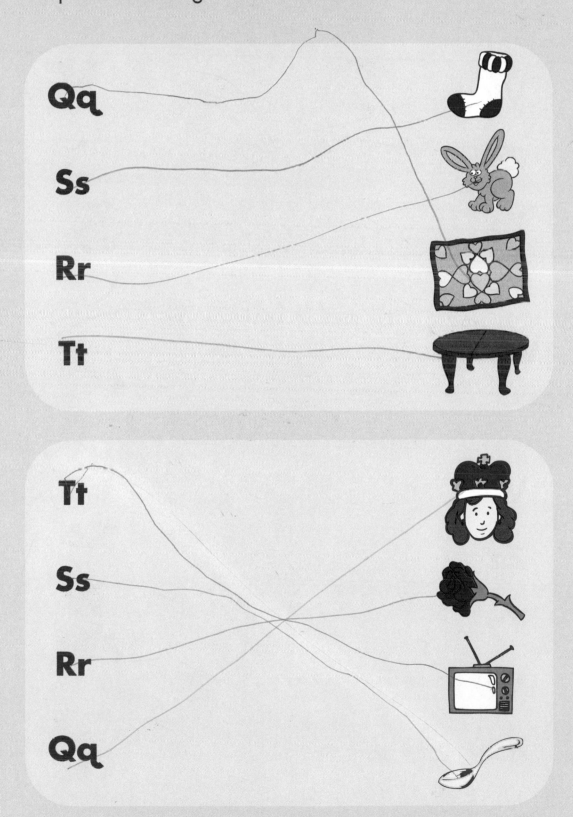

Qq

Ss

Rr

Tt

Tt

Ss

Rr

Qq

Consonant Roundup:
V, W, X, Y, Z

Directions: Say the name of each letter. Say the sound that each letter makes. Then, draw a line from each letter pair to the picture that begins with that sound.

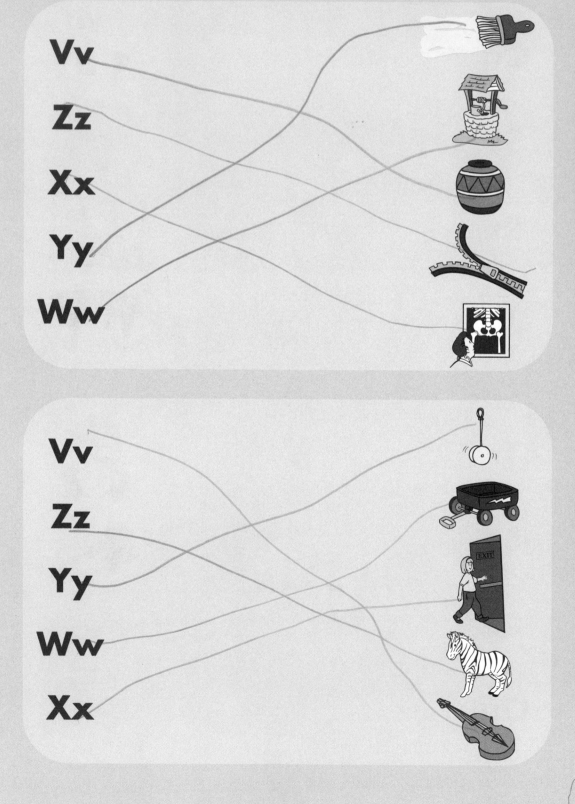

Vv

Zz

Xx

Yy

Ww

Vv

Zz

Yy

Ww

Xx

Review

Directions: Write the letter that makes the beginning sound for each picture.

 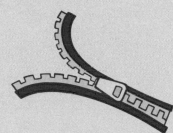 

C ar   Z ipper   K ite

L etter   b oat   r ose

S un   h ouse   T urtle

Consonant Roundup:
b, d, f

Ending Consonants are the sounds that come at the end of words.

Directions: Say the name of each picture. Then, write the letter that makes the **ending** sound for each picture.

Web — b

Knife — f

Sled — bd

Crab — b

bird — d

eaf — f

Wood — cdd

hand — db

roof — f

Consonant Roundup: k, l, p

Directions: Trace the letters in each row. Say the name of each picture. Then, color the pictures in each row that end with that sound.

Consonant Roundup:
r, s, t, x

Directions: Say the name of each picture. Then, circle the ending sound for each picture.

(r) s t x

r (s) t x

(r) s t x

r s (t) x

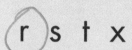

r s (t) x

r (s) t x

r s t (x)

r s (t) x

From Start to Finish

Directions: Say the name of each picture. Write the beginning and ending sounds for each picture.

Say It Short

Vowels are the letters **a**, **e**, **i**, **o** and **u**. Short **a** is the sound you hear in **ant**. Short **e** is the sound you hear in **elephant**. Short **i** is the sound you hear in **igloo**. Short **o** is the sound you hear in **octopus**. Short **u** is the sound you hear in **umbrella**.

Directions: Say the short vowel sound at the beginning of each row. Say the name of each picture. Then, color the pictures that have the same short vowel sounds as that letter.

Say It Short

Directions: In each box are three pictures. The words that name the pictures have missing letters. Write **a, e, i, o** or **u** to finish the words.

p _e_ n

p _i_ n

p _a_ n

b _u_ g

b _a_ g

b _e_ g

c _a_ t

c _o_ t

c _u_ t

h _i_ t

h _a_ t

h _o_ t

Say It Long

Vowels are the letters **a**, **e**, **i**, **o** and **u**. Long vowel sounds say their own names. Long **a** is the sound you hear in **hay**. Long **e** is the sound you hear in **me**. Long **i** is the sound you hear in **pie**. Long **o** is the sound you hear in **no**. Long **u** is the sound you hear in **cute**.

Directions: Say the long vowel sound at the beginning of each row. Say the name of each picture. Color the pictures in each row that have the same long vowel sound as that letter.

Say It Long

Directions: Write **a**, **e**, **i**, **o** or **u** in each blank to finish the word. Draw a line from the word to the picture.

c a ke

r o se

k i te

f ee t

m u le

Letter Detective: Aa

Directions: Each train has a group of pictures. Write the word that names the pictures. Read your rhyming words.

These trains use the short **a** sound like in the word cat:

pan   can   fan   man

rat   cat   bat   hat

These trains use the long **a** sound like in the word lake:

skate   gate   plate

rake   cake   snake

Letter Detective: Aa

Directions: Say the name of each picture. If it has the short **a** sound, color it **red**. If it has the long **a** sound, color it yellow.

ă

ā

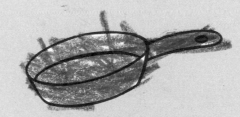

Letter Detective: Ee

Directions: Short **e** sounds like the **e** in **hen**. Long **e** sounds like the **e** in **bee**. Look at the pictures. If the word has a short **e** sound, draw a line to the **hen** with your **red** crayon. If the word has a long **e** sound, draw a line to the **bee** with your **green** crayon.

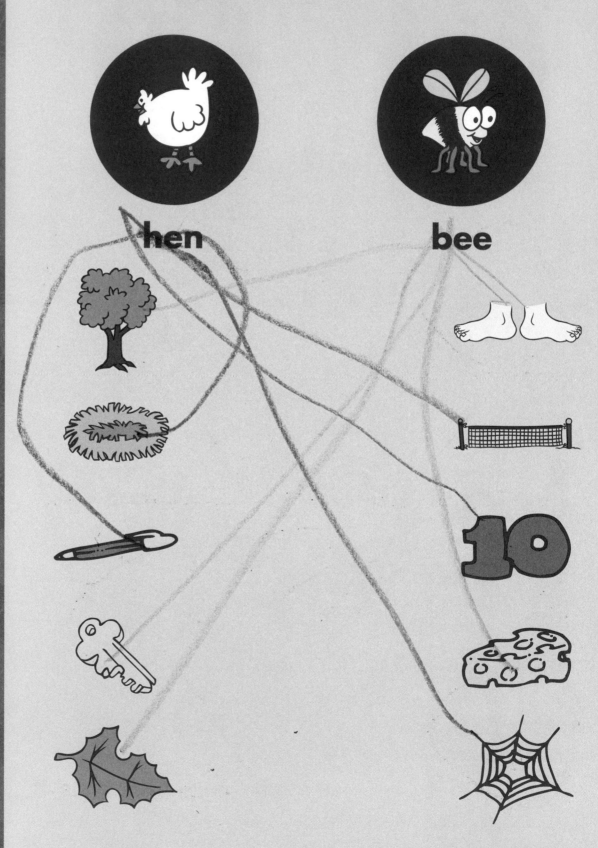

hen

bee

Letter Detective: Ee

Directions: Say the name of each picture. Circle the pictures which have the short **e** sound. Draw a triangle around the pictures which have the long **e** sound.

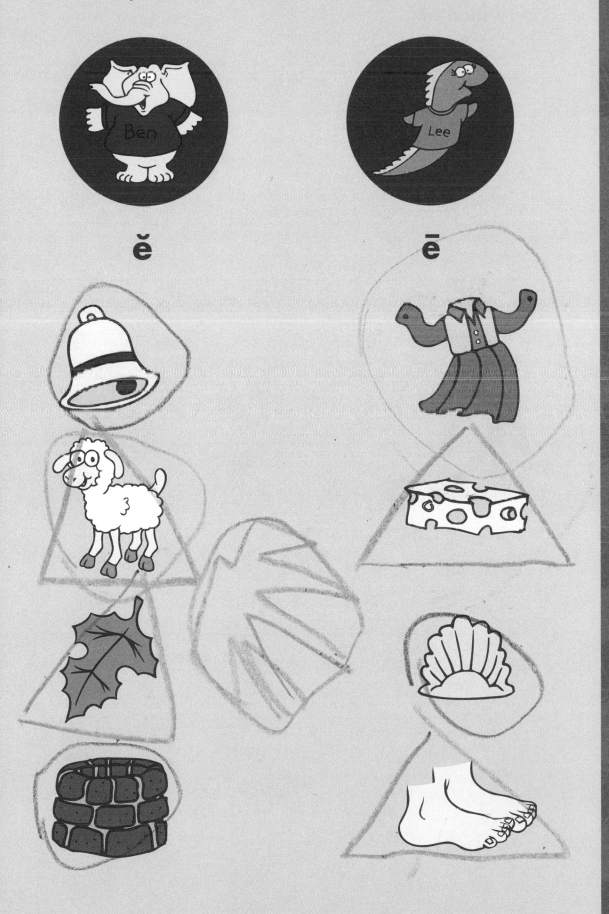

ĕ   ē

Letter Detective: Ii

Directions: Short **i** sounds like the **i** in **pig**. Long **i** sounds like the **i** in **kite**. Draw a circle around the words with the short **i** sound. Draw an **X** on the words with the long **i** sound.

pin

five

pig

slide

kite

lid

tie

bib

pie

Letter Detective: Ii

Directions: Say the name of each picture. If it has a short **i** sound, color it **yellow**. If it has a long **i** sound, color it **red**.

ĭ

ī

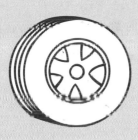

Letter Detective: Oo

Directions: The short **o** sounds like the **o** in **dog**. Long **o** sounds like the **o** in **rope**. Draw a line from the picture to the word that names it. Draw a circle around the word if it has a short **o** sound.

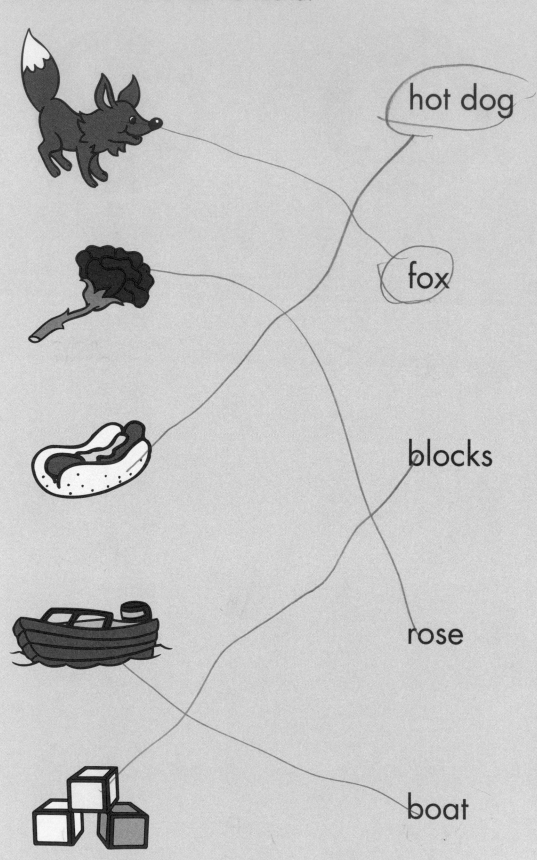

hot dog

fox

blocks

rose

boat

Letter Detective: Oo

Directions: Say the name of each picture. If the picture has the long **o** sound, write a **green L** on the blank. If the picture has the short **o** sound, write a **red S** on the blank.

d_one   log

frog   cloc   smoc

thron   soce   locit

Letter Detective: Uu

Directions: The short **u** sounds like the **u** in **bug**. The long **u** sounds like the **u** in **blue**. Draw a circle around the words with short **u**. Draw an **X** on the words with long **u**.

rug   cup   music

tub   suit   glue

bug   puppy   gum

Letter Detective: Uu

Directions: Say the name of each picture. If it has the short **u** sound, write a **u** in the **umbrella** column. If it has the long **u** sound, write a **u** in the **unicorn** column.

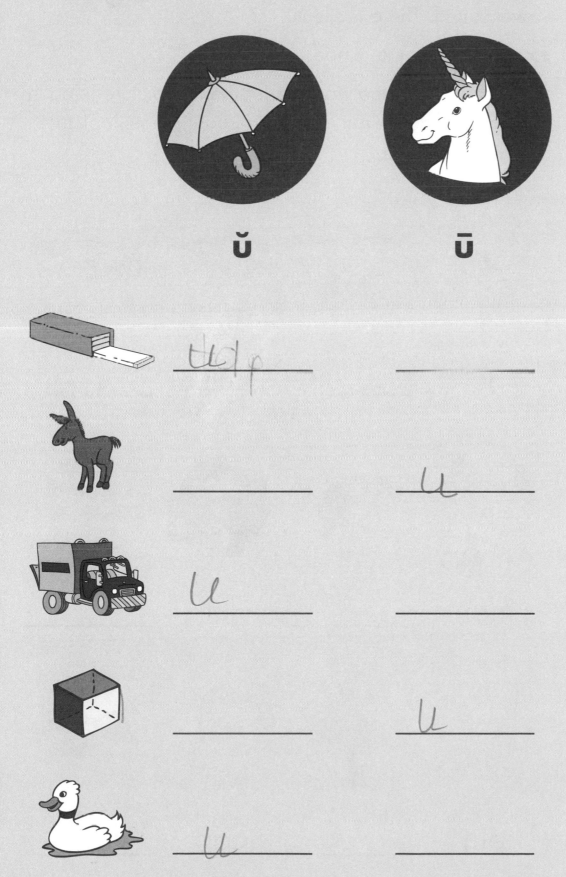

Ŭ   Ū

help	———
_____	u
u	_____
_____	u
u	_____

Super Silent E

When you add an **e** to the end of some words, the vowel changes from a short vowel sound to a long vowel sound. The **e** is silent.

Example: rip + **e** = ripe

Directions: Say the word under the first picture in each pair. Then, add an **e** to the word under the next picture. Say the new word.

pet _dog_   tub _tube_

man _mane_   kit _kite_

pin _pine_   cap _cape_

Sort It Out

Directions: Cut out the pictures below. If the vowel has a **long** sound, glue it on the **long** vowel side. If the vowel has a **short** sound, glue it on the **short** vowel side.

Short	**Long**
h a t bike	boat
bed	bike
pig	cube
pots	beads
truck	cake

Cut ✂

hat · boat · bike · cube · bed

pig · beads · cake · pots · truck

This page is blank for the cutting activity
on the opposite side.

My Vowel List

Keep this list handy and add more words to it.

short a
(ă as in cat)

uN oOoT ToO UU

long a
(ā as in train)

Aa E e T T o o U u

bat

short e
(ě as in get)

pet

long e
(ē as in tree)

bee

short i
(ĭ as in pin)

tin

long i
(ī as in ice)

icey

short o
(ŏ as in cot)

hot

long o
(ō as in boat)

loaf

short u
(ŭ as in cut)

hut

long u
(ū as in cube)

puke

Aa Ee Ii Oo Uu

This page is blank for the activity
on the opposite side.

Review

Directions: Color all of the vowels **black** to discover something hidden in the puzzle.

```
j e j g w d q n j c g c u b
k g u m b j h c h w l a d s
r c z i l p q s b k i n z f
g k w x a d a e f e l x q k
v r f j p i a u a g n f s b
d n v m a e e i u o h b s f
a a a e i e u a i u e a e i u
l z k i i i i i i i i m w z
q h r a a u e i a e e c b
i u e u a o i o o u
t x b h a i e o u a d v r l
c h f s j e i e i f f k j v
n m d t e g a o i i j m x h
t p g i c v h n g d o p r l
l h o k q f r p s j t e g v
```

What was hidden? **spider**

Review

Directions: Write the vowel on each line that completes the word.

a   e   i   o   u

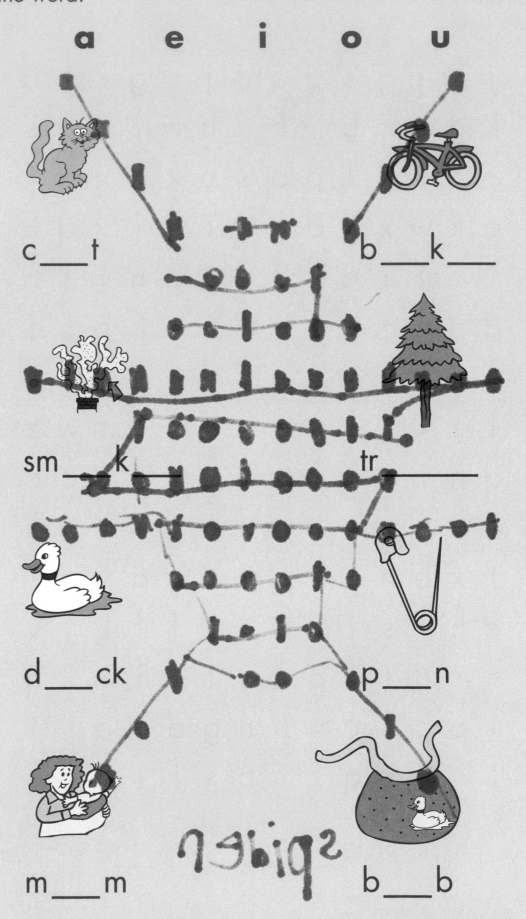

c___t

b___k___

sm___k

tr_____

d___ck

p___n

m___m

b___b

Review

Directions: Circle the **long vowel** words with a **red** crayon. Underline the **short vowel** words with a **blue** crayon.

Remember: The vowel is long if:

- There are two vowels in the word. The first vowel is the sound you hear.

- There is a "super silent e" at the end.

cub	red	coat
bite	cube	cage
cat	mean	rake
bit	cot	hen
leaf	feet	key
pen	web	bee
nest	boat	fox
rose	dog	pig

# Begin with a Blend

Consonant blends are two or more consonant sounds together in a word. The blend is made by combining the consonant sounds.

Example: floor

Directions: The name of each picture begins with a **blend**. Circle the beginning blend for each picture.

bl fl cl   cl fl gl   fl bl pl

fl cl gl   pl gl cl   gl fl sl

gl fl cl   sl fl cl   cl gl sl

Blend in the Blank

Directions: The beginning blend for each word is missing. Fill in the correct blend to finish the word. Draw a line from the word to the picture.

_____ ain

_____ og

_____ um

_____ ush

_____ esent

Find a Blend

Directions: Say the blend for each word as you search for it.

```
b l o s l e d a b f t k a i n
l b r e a d x s t o p i x a p
o l g u f e n p s p i d e r i
c l o w n a w l p z j c r a b
k t c e n t h s t e g l q c r
d h b r e a e j w k x o w h y
h u s n a k e m d j l c m a j
v m i u k l l s k u n k c i f
i b g l o b e m h n o q t r r
b f l j x s y a z s l e d o o
s h e l l w k l f s s v u p g
h a r l c a d l l v w k z s n
o z y q s n l t a h n r u m q
e f l o w e r a g l o v e e r
w g m b c e n m o p d o f l g
p r e s e n t r a i n b p l i
```

Words to find:

block   sled   globe   crab   clock   frog
present   flower   train   glove   skunk   snake
swan   flag   smell   spider   bread   small
chair   shell   stop   sled   shoe   thumb
wheel   clown

Jukebox Jam

Directions: Every jukebox has a word ending and a list of letters. Add each of the letters to the word ending to make rhyming words.

___and

b _____

h _____

l _____

s _____

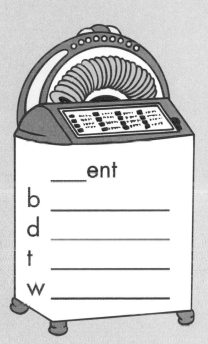

___ent

b _____

d _____

t _____

w _____

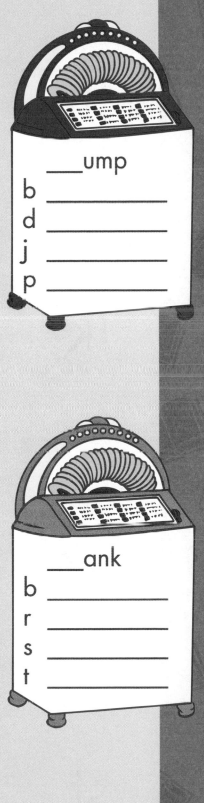

___ump

b _____

d _____

j _____

p _____

___ink

p _____

s _____

l _____

th _____

___ing

r _____

s _____

st _____

k _____

___ank

b _____

r _____

s _____

t _____

End with a Blend

Directions: Draw a line from the picture to the blend that ends the word.

lf

lk

sk

st

Review

Directions: Finish each sentence with a word from the word box.

sting   shelf   drank   plant   stamp

1. Tom _____ his milk.

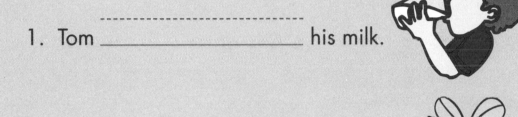

2. A bee can _____ you.

3. I put a _____ on my letter.

4. The _____ is green.

5. The book is on the _____ .

Rhythm and Rhyme

Rhyming words are words that sound alike at the end of the word. **Cat** and **hat** rhyme.

Directions: Draw a circle around each word pair that rhymes. Draw an **X** on each pair that does not rhyme.

Example:

soap rope	red dog	book hook

cold rock	cat hat	yellow black

one two	rock sock	rat flat

good nice	you to	meet toy

old sold	sale whale	word letter

Rhythm and Rhyme

Rhyming words are words that sound alike at the end of the word.

Directions: Draw a line to match the pictures that rhyme. Write two of your rhyming word pairs below.

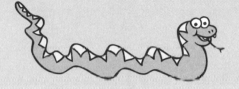

_____   _____

_____   _____

A, B, C Dinosaur

Directions: Abc order is the order in which letters come in the alphabet. Draw a line to connect the dots. Follow the letters in **abc** order. Then, color the picture.

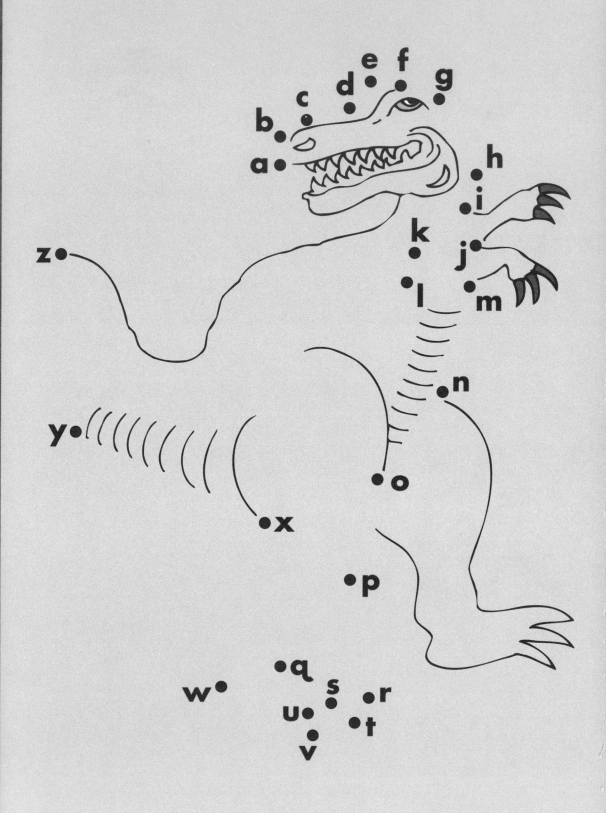

Putting Things in Order

Directions: Circle the first letter of each word. Then, put each pair of words in abc order.

ⓒar   ⓑird   moon   **2** two

bird

car

nest   fan   card   dog

pig   bike   sun   pie

Two Words in One

Compound words are two words that are put together to make one new word.

Directions: Look at the pictures and the two words that are next to each other. Put the words together to make a new word. Write the new word.

Example:

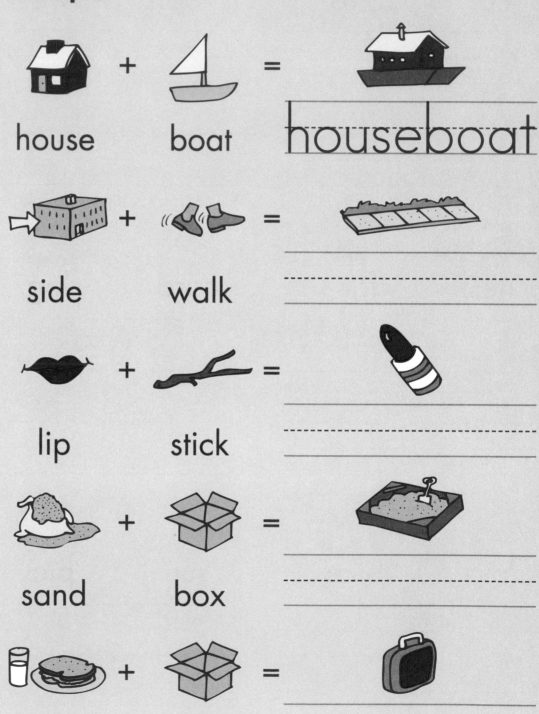

house + boat = houseboat

side walk _____

lip stick _____

sand box _____

lunch box _____

Double the Fun

Directions: Cut out the cards below. Turn them over. Take turns trying to make compound words. When a compound word is made, the player gets to keep the word.

Cut ✂

flash	snow	ball	sun
mail	house	plant	room
light	bow	light	card
base	shine	dog	box
rain	flake	thing	post
family	house	in	house
any	side	day	birth

This page is blank for the cutting activity
on the opposite side.

The Name Game

You are a special person. Your name begins with a capital letter. We put a capital letter at the beginning of people's names because they are special.

Directions: Write your name. Did you remember to use a capital letter?

_____

- -

_____

Directions: Write each person's name. Use a capital letter at the beginning.

Ted _____

Katie _____

Marcos _____

Tim _____

Write a friend's name. Use a capital letter at the beginning.

_____

- -

7 Delightful Days

The days of the week begin with capital letters.

Directions: Write the days of the week in the spaces below. Put them in order. Be sure to start with capital letters.

Tuesday _____

Saturday _____

Monday _____

Friday _____

Thursday _____

Sunday _____

Wednesday _____

12 Marvelous Months

The months of the year begin with capital letters.

Directions: Write the months of the year in order on the calendar below. Be sure to use capital letters.

January	December	April	May
October	June	September	February
July	March	November	August

Little Riddles

Directions: Read the word and write it on the line. Then, read each riddle and draw a line to the picture and word that tells about it.

house

_____

I like to play.
I am little. I am soft.
What am I?

kitten

_____

I am big.
People live in me.
What am I?

flower

_____

I am pretty.
I am green and yellow.
What am I?

pony

_____

I can jump. I can run.
I am brown
What am I?

Get the Picture?

Directions: Read the sentence. Circle the word that makes sense. Use the picture clues to help you. Then, write the word.

I ride on a _____ .

bike   **hike**

I ride on a _____ .

train   **tree**

I ride in a _____ .

car   **can**

I ride on a _____ .

bus   **bug**

I ride in a _____ .

jar   **jet**

I ride in a _____ .

took   **truck**

Winter Warmers

Directions: Color the things that keep you warm.

socks

apple

lunch box

earmuffs

cookie

hat

coat

umbrella

gloves

Sunlight, Moonlight

Directions: Write the words from the box under the pictures they describe.

stars   sun   moon   rays

dark   light   night   day

Like It or Not

Directions: Circle the picture in each row that is most like the first picture.

Example:

 **carrot**

 jacks   bread    pea

 baseball

 sneakers   basketball   bat

 store

 school   home   bakery

 kitten

 dog   fox   cat

Odd One Out

Directions: Draw an **X** on the picture that does not belong in each group.

fruit

| apple | peach | corn | watermelon |

wild animals

| bear | kitten | gorilla | lion |

pets

| cat | fish | elephant | dog |

flowers

| grass | rose | daisy | tulip |

See It, Sort It

Directions: Write each word in the correct row at the bottom of the page.

airplane   plate   car

pencil   spoon   crayon

chalk   fork   boat

Things we ride in:

_____

_____

Things we eat with:

_____

_____

Things we draw with:

_____

_____

Time to Rhyme

Directions: Circle the pictures in each row that rhyme.

Row 1

Row 2

Row 3

Directions: Write the names of the pictures that do not rhyme.

These words do not rhyme:

Row 1   Row 2   Row 3

_____   _____   _____

_____   _____   _____

Twice the Fun!

Directions: Read the story. Then, use the words in the box and the picture to write your answers.

Ben and Ann are twin babies. They were born at the same time. They have the same mother. Ben is a boy baby. Ann is a girl baby.

mother   bow   boy   girl   hat   twins

1. Tell one way Ann and Ben are the same.

_____

_____

----

2. Ann and Ben are _____.

3. Tell two ways Ann and Ben are different.

_____   _____

----------------------   ----------------------

Ann is a _____. Ben is a _____.

Ann is wearing a _____.

Ben is wearing a _____.

Map It!

Directions: Color the path the girl should take to go home. Use the sentences to help you.

1. Go to the school and turn left.

2. At the end of the street, turn right.

3. Walk past the park and turn right.

4. After you pass the pool, turn right.

Make a Snowman!

Directions: Write the number of the sentence that goes with each picture in the circle.

1. Roll a large snowball for the snowman's bottom.

2. Make another snowball and put it on top of the first.

3. Put the last snowball on top.

4. Dress the snowman.

How Does Your Garden Grow?

Directions: Read the story. Then, write the steps to grow a flower.

First find a sunny spot. Then, plant the seed. Water it. The flower will start to grow. Pull the weeds around it. Remember to keep giving the flower water. Enjoy your flower.

1. _____

2. _____

3. _____

4. _____

5. _____

On the Pond

Directions: Look at the picture. Write the words from the box to finish the sentences.

frog   log   bird   fish   ducks

The _____ can jump.

The turtle is on a _____ .

A _____ is in the tree.

The boy wants a _____ .

I see three _____ .

An Apple a Day

Directions: Read about apples. Then, write the answers.

I like  . Do you?

Some  are red.

Some  are green.

Some  are yellow.

1. How many kinds of apples does the story tell about?
   _____
   -
   _____

2. Name the kinds of apples.
   _____ _____ _____
   - - - - - - - - - - - - - - - - - - - - - - - - - - -
   _____ _____ _____

3. What kind of apple do you like best?
   _____
   -
   _____

Puddle Jumping

Directions: Read the story. Write the words from the story that complete each sentence.

Jada and Bill like to play in the rain. They take off their shoes and socks. They splash in the puddles. It feels cold! It is fun to splash!

Jada and Bill like to _____ .

They take off their _____ .

They splash in _____ .

Do you like to splash in puddles?   Yes   No

Falling Leaves

Directions: Read about raking leaves. Then, answer the questions.

I like to rake leaves. Do you? Leaves die each year. They get brown and dry. They fall from the trees. Then, we rake them up.

1. What color are leaves when they die?

   _____

   _____

2. What happens when they die?

   _____

   _____

   _____

   _____

3. What do we do when leaves fall?

   _____

   _____

Bunches of Balloons

Directions: Read the story. Then, answer the questions.

Some balloons float. They are filled with gas. Some do not float. They are filled with air. Some clowns carry balloons. Balloons come in many colors. What color do you like?

1. What makes balloons float? _____

2. What is in balloons that do not float? _____

3. What shape are the balloons the clown is holding? _____

Time to Party!

Directions: Read about the party. Then, complete the invitation.

   The party will be at Dog's house. The party will start at 1:00 P.M. It will last 2 hours. Write your birthday for the date of the party.

Party Invitation

Where: _____

Date: _____

Time It Begins: _____

Time It Ends: _____

_____

Directions: On the last line, write something else about the party.

Review

Directions: Read the story. Then, circle the pictures of things that are wet.

Some things used in baking are dry. Some things used in baking are wet. To bake a cake, first mix the salt, sugar and flour. Then, add the egg. Now, add the milk. Stir. Put the cake in the oven.

Directions: Tell the order to mix things when you bake a cake.

1. _____

2. _____

3. _____

4. _____

5. _____

Directions: Circle the answers.

6. The first things to mix are   dry   wet.

7. Where are cakes baked?   oven   grill

A Tiger Tale

Directions: Read about tigers. Then, write the answers.

Tigers sleep during the day. They hunt at night. Tigers eat meat. They hunt deer. They like to eat wild pigs. If they cannot find meat, tigers will eat fish.

1. When do tigers sleep?

   _____

   _____

2. Name two things tigers eat.

   _____

   _____

   _____

   _____

3. When do tigers hunt?

   _____

   _____

Get a Clue

Directions: Read the story about tigers again. Then, complete the puzzle.

Across

1. When tigers cannot get meat, they eat _____.

3. The food tigers like best is _____.

4. Tigers like to eat this meat: wild _____.

Down

2. Tigers do this during the day.

Tiger Art

Directions: Follow directions to complete the picture of the tiger.

1. Draw **black** stripes on the tiger's body and tail.

2. Color the tiger's tongue **red**.

3. Draw claws on the feet.

4. Draw a **black** nose and two **black** eyes on the tiger's face.

5. Color the rest of the tiger orange.

6. Draw tall, green grass for the tiger to sleep in.

Simon Says

Directions: Read how to play Simon Says. Then, answer the questions.

Simon Says

Here is how to play Simon Says: One kid is Simon. Simon is the leader. Everyone must do what Simon says and does but only if the leader says, "Simon says" first. Let's try it. "Simon says, 'Pat your head.'" "Simon says, 'Pat your nose. Pat your toes.'" Oops! Did you pat your toes? I did not say, "Simon says," first. If you patted your toes, you are out!

1. Who is the leader in this game?

   _____

   _____

2. What must the leader say first each time?

   _____

   _____

3. What happens if you do something and the leader did not say, "Simon says"?

   _____

   _____

Eyes on Simon

Directions: Read each sentence. Look at the picture next to it. Circle the picture if the person is playing Simon Says correctly.

1. Simon says, "Put your hands on your hips."

2. Simon says, "Stand on one leg."

3. Simon says, "Put your hands on your head."

4. Simon says, "Ride a bike."

5. Simon says, "Jump up and down."

6. Simon says, "Pet a dog."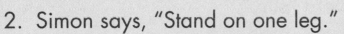

A Message from Simon

Directions: Read the sentences. If Simon tells you to do something, follow the directions. If Simon does not tell you to do something, go to the next sentence.

1. Simon says: Cross out all the numbers 2 through 9.

2. Simon says: Cross out the vowel that is in the word "sun."

3. Cross out the letter "B."

4. Cross out the vowels "A" and "E."

5. Simon says: Cross out the consonants in the word "cup."

6. Cross out the letter "Z."

7. Simon says: Cross out all the "K's."

8. Simon says: Read your message.

C 3 G U 7 P R U C P E K C P A 8 K K
6 T P U P J C 5 P O K 9 P B U P K K

Boats Afloat

Directions: Read about boats. Then, answer the questions.

See the boats! They float on water. Some boats have sails. The wind moves the sails. It makes the boats go. Many people name their sailboats. They paint the name on the side of the boat.

1. What makes sailboats move?

   _____

   _____

2. Where do sailboats float?

   _____

   _____

3. What would you name a sailboat?

   _____

Sail Away

Directions: Find the three boats that are alike. Color them all the same. One boat is different. Color it differently.

Gone to Sea

Directions: Write a sentence under each picture to tell what is happening. Read the story you wrote.

_____

- -

_____

_____

- -

_____

_____

- -

_____

_____

- -

_____

_____

- -

_____

_____

- -

_____

What's Next?

Directions: Complete each story by choosing the correct picture. Draw a line from the story to the picture.

1. Shawnda got her books. She went to the bus stop. Shawnda got on the bus.

2. Marco planted a seed. He watered it. He pulled the weeds around it.

3. Abraham's dog was barking. Abraham got out the dog food. He put it in the dog bowl.

A Happy Ending

Directions: Read each story. Circle the sentence that tells how the story will end.

Ann was riding her bike. She saw a dog in the park. She stopped to pet it. Ann left to go home.

The dog went swimming.

The dog followed Ann.

The dog went home with a cat.

Antonio went to a baseball game. A baseball player hit a ball toward him. He reached out his hands.

The player caught the ball.

The ball bounced on a car.

Antonio caught the ball.

How Would You Feel?

Directions: Read each story. Choose a word from the box to show how each person feels.

> happy   excited   sad   mad

1. Andy and Sam were best friends. Sam and his family moved far away. How does Sam feel?

   _____

   _____

2. Deana could not sleep. It was the night before her birthday party. How does Deana feel?

   _____

   _____

3. Jacob let his baby brother play with his teddy bear. His brother lost the bear. How does Jacob feel?

   _____

   _____

4. Kia picked flowers for her mom. Her mom smiled when she got them. How does Kia feel?

   _____

   _____

English

Nouns All Around

Directions: Write these naming words in the correct box.

store   zoo   child   baby
teacher   table   cat   park
gym   woman   sock   horse

Person

_____   _____

_____   _____

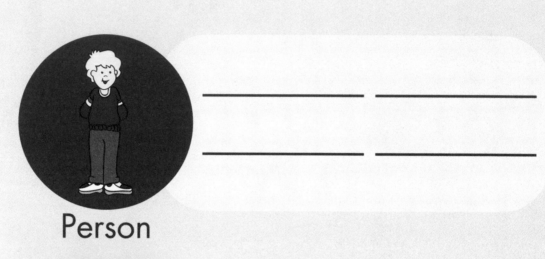
Place

_____   _____

_____   _____

Thing

_____   _____

_____   _____

Pick a Pair

Some nouns name things that go together.

Directions: Draw a line to match the nouns on the left with the things they go with on the right.

toothpaste

washcloth

pencil

sock

salt

toothbrush

shoe

pepper

soap

paper

pillow

bed

Get in on the Action

Directions: Look at the picture and read the words. Write an action word in each sentence below.

swing   rings

kick

run   talk

1. The two boys like to _____ together.

2. The children _____ the soccer ball.

3. Some children like to _____ on the swing.

4. The girl can _____ very fast.

5. The teacher _____ the bell.

Review

Directions: Read the sentences below. Draw a **red** circle around the nouns. Draw a **blue** line under the verbs.

1. The boy runs fast.

2. The turtle eats leaves.

3. The fish swim in the tank.

4. The girl hits the ball.

Show and Tell

Directions: Read the words in the box. Choose the word that describes the picture. Write it next to the picture.

wet   round   funny   soft   sad   tall

 _____

 _____

 _____

 _____

 _____

 _____

Picture Perfect

Colors and numbers can describe nouns.

Directions: Underline the describing word in each sentence. Draw a picture to go with each sentence.

A yellow moon was in the sky.

Two worms are on the road.

The tree had red apples.

The girl wore a blue dress.

1, 2, 3—Compare and See

Directions: Look at the pictures in each row. Write 1, 2 or 3 under the picture to show where it should be.

Example:

tallest __3__   tall __1__   taller __2__

small _____   smallest _____   smaller _____

biggest _____   big _____   bigger _____

wider _____   wide _____   widest _____

1, 2, 3—Compare and See

Directions: Look at the pictures in each row. Write 1, 2 or 3 under the picture to show where it should be.

shortest _____   shorter _____   short _____

longest _____   longer _____   long _____

happy _____   happier _____   happiest _____

hotter _____   hot _____   hottest _____

Synonym Sense

Synonyms are words that mean almost the same thing. **Start** and **begin** are synonyms.

Directions: Find the synonyms that describe each picture. Write the words in the boxes below the picture.

small funny large sad
silly little big unhappy

_____ _____

_____ _____

_____ _____

_____ _____

Two of a Kind

Directions: Circle the word in each row that is most like the first word in the row.

Example:

 grin

(smile)   frown   mad

 **bag**

jar   sack   box

 **cat**

fruit   animal   flower

 apple

rot   cookie   fruit

 around

circle   square   dot

 **bird**

dog   cat   duck

A Synonym Story

Directions: Read the story. Write a word on the line that means almost the same as the word under the line.

Dan went to the _____ .
store

He wanted to buy _____ .
food

He walked very _____ .
quickly

The store had what he wanted.

He bought it using _____ .
dimes

Instead of walking home, Dan _____ .
jogged

All About Antonyms

Antonyms are words that are opposites. **Hot** and **cold** are antonyms.

Directions: Draw a line between the antonyms.

closed

below

full

empty

above

old

new

open

Opposites Attract

Directions: Circle the picture in each row that is the opposite of the first picture.

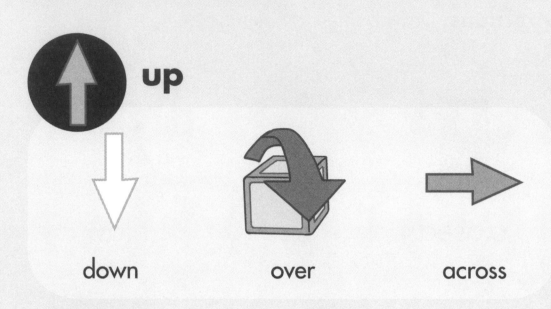

up

down   over   across

cold

frozen   hot   warm

cloud

rain   storm   sun

Fishing for Antonyms

Directions: Read each clue. Write the answers in the puzzle.

high   yes   left
heavy   tight
safe   full

Across:

1. Opposite of low

2. Opposite of no

4. Opposite of empty

6. Opposite of loose

Down:

1. Opposite of light

3. Opposite of dangerous

5. Opposite of right

Sound Alikes

Homophones are words that **sound** the same but are spelled differently and mean something different. **Blew** and **blue** are homophones.

Directions: Look at the word pairs. Choose the word that describes the picture. Write the word on the line next to the picture.

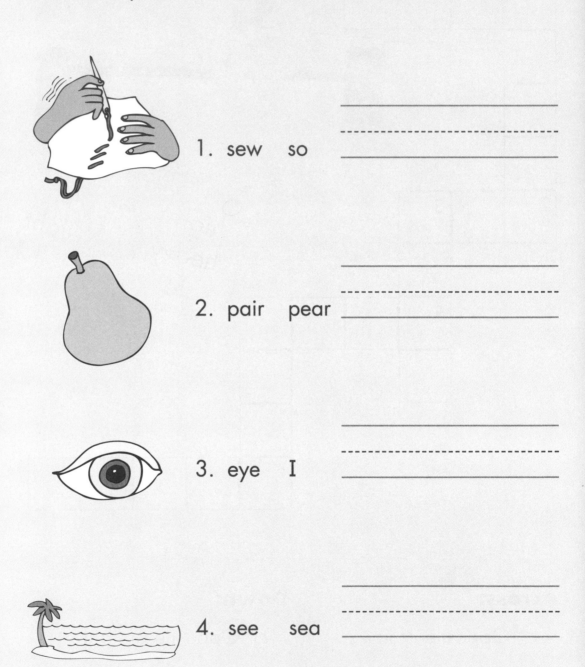

1. sew   so   _____

2. pair   pear   _____

3. eye   I   _____

4. see   sea   _____

Sound Alikes

Directions: Read each sentence. Underline the two words that sound the same but are spelled differently and mean something different.

1. Tom ate eight grapes.

2. Becky read *Little Red Riding Hood*.

3. I went to buy two dolls.

4. Five blue feathers blew in the wind.

5. Would you get wood for the fire?

Say it with a Sentence

Sentences begin with capital letters.

Directions: Read the sentences and write them below. Begin each sentence with a capital letter.

Example:

the cat is fat.

The cat is fat.

my dog is big.

the boy is sad.

bikes are fun!

dad can bake.

All in Order

If you change the order of the words in a sentence, you can change the meaning of a sentence.

Directions: Read the sentences. Draw a circle around the sentence that describes the picture.

Example:

The fox jumped over the dogs.

The dogs jumped over the fox.

1. The cat watched the bird.

   The bird watched the cat.

2. The girl looked at the boy.

   The boy looked at the girl.

3. The turtle ran past the rabbit.

   The rabbit ran past the turtle.

Lemonade for Sale!

Directions: Look at the picture. Put the words in order. Write the sentences on the lines below.

1. We made lemonade. some

2. good. It was

3. We the sold lemonade.

4. cost It five cents.

5. fun. We had

1. _____

2. _____

3. _____

4. _____

5. _____

Telling Sentences: Pet Crazy

Directions: Read the sentences and write them below. Begin each sentence with a capital letter. End each sentence with a period.

1. most children like pets
2. some children like dogs
3. some children like cats
4. some children like snakes
5. some children like all animals

1. _____

2. _____

3. _____

4. _____

5. _____

Telling Sentences: Going Shopping

Directions: Read the sentences and write them below. Begin each sentence with a capital letter. End each sentence with a period.

1. i like to go to the store with Mom
2. we go on Friday
3. i get to push the cart
4. i get to buy the cookies
5. I like to help Mom

1. _____

2. _____

3. _____

4. _____

5. _____

Asking Sentences: Monkeying Around

Directions: Write the first word of each asking sentence. Be sure to begin each question with a capital letter. End each question with a question mark.

1. _____ you like the zoo   **do**

2. _____ much does it cost   **how**

3. _____ you feed the ducks   **can**

4. _____ you see the monkeys   **will**

5. _____ time will you eat lunch   **what**

Asking Sentences: Getting to Know You

Directions: Read the asking sentences. Write the sentences below. Begin each sentence with a capital letter. End each sentence with a question mark.

1. what game will we play

2. do you like to read

3. how old are you

4. who is your best friend

5. can you tie your shoes

1. _____

2. _____

3. _____

4. _____

5. _____

Punctuation Parade

Directions: Put a period or a question mark at the end of each sentence below.

1. Do you like parades

2. The clowns lead the parade

3. Can you hear the band

4. The balloons are big

5. Can you see the horses

Review

Directions: Look at the picture. In the space below, write one telling sentence about the picture. Then, write one asking sentence about the picture.

Telling sentence:

_____

_____

Asking sentence:

_____

_____

Spelling

It's a Colorful World

Directions: Use the color words to complete these sentences. Then, put a period at the end.

Example:

My new are _____orange_ .

green tree   blue bike   yellow chick   red ball

1. The baby  is _____ ☐

2. This is _____ ☐

3. My is big and _____ ☐

4. My sister's is _____ ☐

Finish the Pictures

Directions: Read the words. Finish the pictures.

a red ball

a black hat

a yellow sun

a pink kite

an orange balloon

a blue umbrella

Mixed-Up Animals

Directions: The letters in the name of each animal are mixed-up. Write each word correctly.

Example:

g f o r   frog

t a c   _____

o d g   _____

i f s h   _____

d i b r   _____

Busy, Busy Animals

Directions: Use the words in the pictures to write a sentence about each animal. Put a period at the end of each sentence.

Example:

The 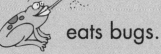 eats bugs.

The  drinks milk

_____

The eats seeds

_____

The jumps out

_____

The meet

_____

From Here to There

Directions: Trace the letters to write the name of each thing. Write each name again by yourself. Then, color the pictures.

Example:

car   car

truck

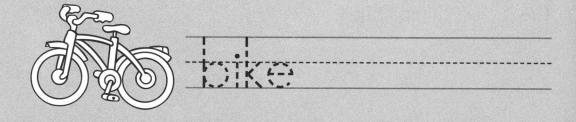

train

bike

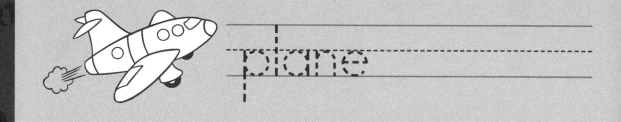

plane

On the Go

Directions: Say the name of each thing. Write the beginning sound under its name. Find two pictures in each row that begin with the same sound as the first picture. Write the same first letter under them.

Example:

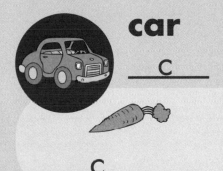 **car**
_____ C _____

_____ C _____   _____ _____   _____ C _____

 train
_____ _____

_____ _____   _____ _____   _____ _____

bike
_____ _____

_____ _____   _____ _____   _____ _____

 **plane**
_____ _____

_____ _____   _____ _____   _____ _____

Time to Get Dressed

Directions: Trace the letters to write the name of each clothing word. Then, write each name again by yourself.

Example:

shirt   shirt

pants

jacket

socks

shoes

dress

Matching Clothes

Directions: Some of these sentences tell a whole idea. Others have something missing. If something is missing, draw a line to the word that completes the sentence. Put a period at the end of each sentence.

Example:

She is wearing a polka-dot

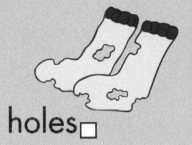

holes ☐

1. The baseball player wore a

2. His pants were torn.

dress ☐

3. The socks had

4. The jacket had blue buttons.

hat ☐

5. The shoes were brown.

A Bite to Eat

Directions: Trace the letters to write the name of each food word. Write each name again by yourself. Then, color the pictures.

Example:

 bread bread

 cookie

 apple

 cake

 milk

 egg

What's for Lunch?

Directions: Write the food names in the story.

Kim got up in the morning.

"Do you want an _____ ?"
  her mother asked.

"Yes, please," Kim said.

"May I have some _____  , too?"

"Okay," her mother said.

"How about some _____  ?"
  Kim asked with a smile.

Her mother laughed. "Not now," she said.

She put an _____ in Kim's lunch.

"Do you want a _____ or some

_____ today?"

"Both!" Kim said.

1, 2, 3 Spell!

Directions: Trace the letters to write the name of each number. Write the numbers again by yourself. Then, color the number pictures.

Example:

1   one   one

2   two

3   three

4   four

5   five

6   six

7   seven

8   eight

9   nine

10   ten

How Many?

Directions: Use the number words to answer each question.

1. How many eyes do you have?

_____

- -

_____

2. How many mouths do you have?

_____

- -

_____

3. How many fingers do you have?

_____

- -

_____

4. How many wheels are on a car?

_____

- -

_____

5. How many peas are in the pod?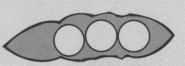

_____

- -

_____

6. How many cups do you see?

_____

- -

_____

Spelling in Action

Directions: Circle the word that is spelled correctly. Then, write the correct spelling in the blank.

Example:

seep

(sleep)

slep

sleep

paly

pay

play

seee

cee

see

rum

run

runn

jump

jumb

junp

Spelling in Action

To show more than one of something, add **s** to the end of the word.

Example: one cat two cats

Directions: In each sentence, add **s** to show more than one. Then, write the action word that completes each sentence.

sit   jump   stop   ride

Example:

The frog ___s___ __sleep__ in the sun.

1. The boy ___ _____ on the fence.

2. The car ___ _____ at the sign.

3. The girl ___ _____ in the water.

4. The dog ___ _____ in the wagon.

Makes Sense to Me!

Directions: Circle the word that is spelled correctly. Then, write the correct spelling in the blank.

Example:

tast

(taste)   -------- taste

tste

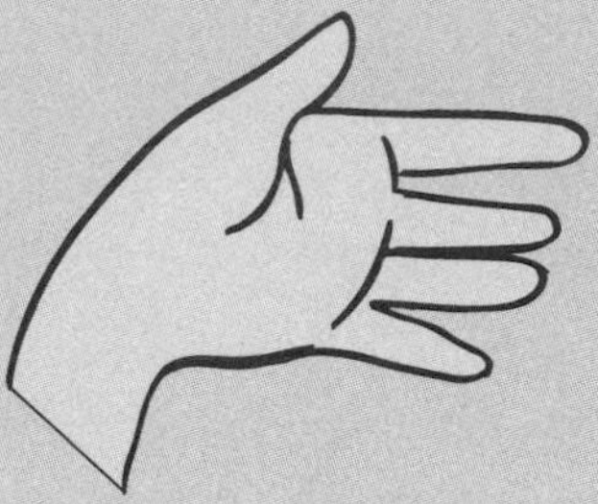

touch

tuch   ----------------------

touh

smel

smll   ----------------------

smell

her

hear   ----------------------

har

see

se   ----------------------

sea

Makes Sense to Me!

Directions: Use the sense words in the box to answer each question.

smell   see   taste   hear   touch

1. Which word begins with the same sound as 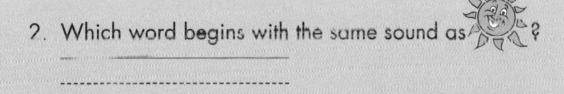?

   _____

   -

   _____

2. Which word begins with the same sound as 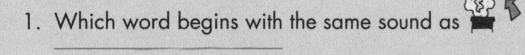?

   _____

   -

   _____

3. Which words begin with the same sound as ?

   _____   _____

   - - - - - - - - - - - -   - - - - - - - - - - - -

   _____   _____

4. Which word begins with the same sound as 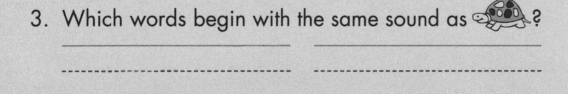?

   _____

   -

   _____

How's the Weather?

Directions: Write the weather word that completes each sentence. Put a period at the end of the telling sentences and a question mark at the end of the asking sentences.

Example:

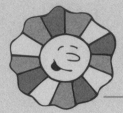

Do flowers grow in the _____ sun _____ ?

rain   water   wet   hot

1. The sun makes me _____ ☐

2. When it rains, the grass gets _____ ☐

3. Do you think it will _____
   on our picnic ☐

4. Should you drink the _____
   from the rain ☐

How's the Weather?

Directions: Write the missing words to complete the story. The first letter of each word is written for you.

"Please may I go outside?" I asked.

"It's too **c**_____," my father told me. "Maybe

later the sun will come out." Later, the sun did come out.

Then, it began to **r**_____ again. "May I go

out now?" I asked again. Dad looked out the window.

"You will get **w**_____," he said. "But I want to

see if the **r**_____ helped our flowers grow,"

I said. "You mean you want to play in the **w**_____,"

Dad said with a smile. How did Dad know that?

Head to Toe

Directions: Write the word that completes each sentence. Put a period at the end of the telling sentences and a question mark at the end of the asking sentences.

Example:

I wear my hat on my ___head___.

arms   legs   feet   hands

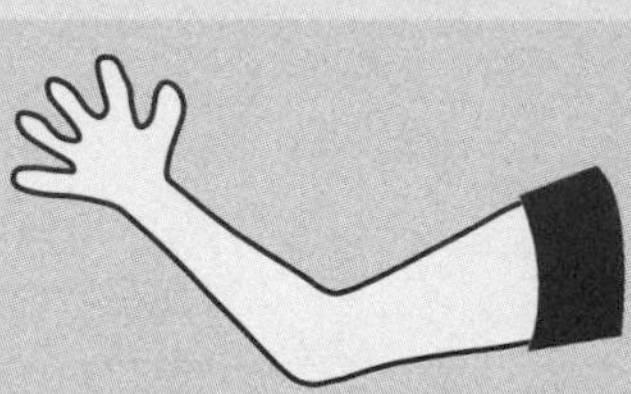

1. How strong are your _____

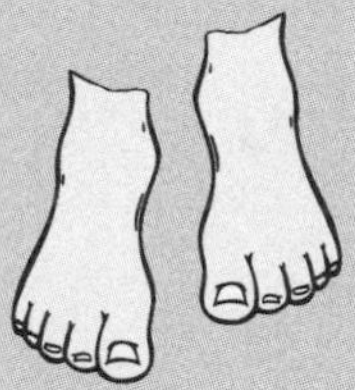

2. You wear shoes on your _____

3. If you're happy and you know it, clap your _____

4. My pants covered my _____

Head to Toe

Directions: Read the sentence parts below. Draw a line from the first part of the sentence to the second part that completes it.

1. I give big hugs

   with my arms.

   with my car.

2. My feet

   drive the car.

   got wet in the rain.

3. I have a bump

   on my head.

   on my coat.

4. My mittens

   keep my arms warm.

   keep my hands warm.

5. I can jump high

   using my legs.

   using a spoon.

What's the Difference?

Some words are opposites. **Opposites** are things that are different in every way. **Dark** and **light** are opposites.

Directions: Trace the letters to write each word. Then, write the word again by yourself.

Example:

new   new

old

big

little

lost

found

What's the Difference?

Directions: Read the sentence about the first picture. Write another sentence about the picture beside it. Use the opposite words.

Example:

This apple is little.

 This apple is big.

dark   old   first   new   light   last

1. This coat is light.

_____

_____

2. This woman is first.

_____

_____

3. This car is old.

_____

_____

People Power!

Directions: Trace the letters to write each word. Then, write the word again by yourself.

girl

boy

man

woman

people

children

People Power!

Sometimes we use other words in place of people names. For **boy** or **man**, we can use the word **he**. For **girl** or **woman**, we can use the word **she**. For two or more people, we can use the word **they**.

Directions: Write the words **he**, **she**, or **they** in these sentences.

Example:

The boy likes cookies.  likes cookies.

1. The girl is running fast.

   _____

   _____ is running fast.

2. The man reads the paper.

   _____

   _____ reads the paper.

3. The woman has a cold.

   _____

   _____ has a cold.

4. Two children came to school.

   _____

   _____ came to school.

SPELLING

People Power!

Directions: Write the people word that completes each sentence.

man   girl   children   boy   woman

1. The _____ feeds the cat.

2. The _____ are buying dessert.

3. What is the _____ painting?

4. The _____ will grow corn.

5. The dog runs to the _____ .

Math

Know Your Numbers

Directions: Use the color codes to color the parrot.

Color:

1's **red**

2's **blue**

3's yellow

4's green

5's orange

Hop to It!

Directions: How many are there of each picture? Write the answers in the boxes. The first one is done for you.

7

Counting Zoo

Directions: How many are there of each shape? Write the answers in the boxes. The first one is done for you.

1

Number Hunt

Directions: Find the number words 0 through 12 hidden in the box.

```
t e a z w z x a b i g t e n
o l z r b e r e v e d l a j
t w e l v e a b o n e c d z
i a r p q d p s u j x e i w
c f o p l s c k i q u i i o
m s t f v i o e t t f g h d
t n u w u x g z w h g h r o
n i n e k f d f o u r t j f
a s g l q c w k o s n v m i
n y c e b o n h h p o m p v
b e x v s s e v e n w e n e
t h r e e r t a l j k x q z
m o a n e n i m u t w a y x
```

Words to find:

zero	four	eight	eleven
one	five	nine	twelve
two	six	ten	
three	seven		

Review

Directions: Match the correct number of objects with the number. Then, match the number with the word.

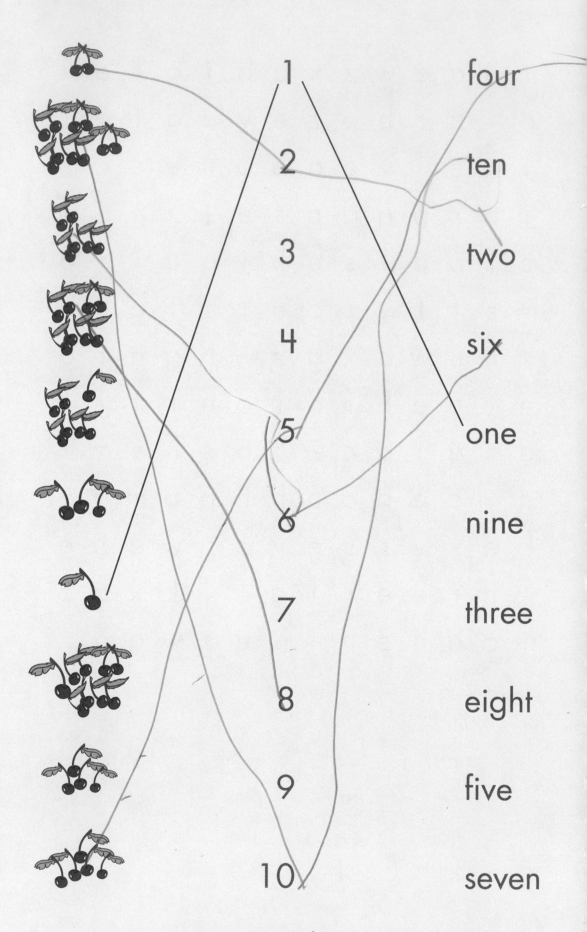

Mix and Match

Directions: Cut out the pictures and number words below. Mix them up and match them again.

Cut ✂

one		two	eight
		five	
	three		nine
four		seven	
	six		ten

This page is blank for the cutting activity on the opposite side.

Following Orders

Sequencing is putting numbers in the correct order.

1, 2, 3, 4, 5, 6, 7, 8, 9, 10

Directions: Write the missing numbers.

Example: 4, ___5___, 6

3, _____, 5   7, _____, 9   8, _____, 10

6, _____, 8   _____, 3, 4   _____, 5, 6

5, 6, _____   _____, 6, 7   _____, 3, 4

_____, 4, 5   _____, 7, 8   5, _____, 7

2, 3, _____   1, 2, _____   7, 8, _____

2, _____, 4   _____, 2, 3   4, _____, 6

Review

Directions: Count the objects and write the number.

_____ _____ _____
--------------------- --------------------- ---------------------
_____ _____ _____

Directions: Match the number to the word.

two	1
four	9
seven	2
three	3
one	4
nine	7

Ordinal Animals

Ordinal numbers are used to indicate order in a series, such as **first**, **second** or **third**.

Directions: Draw a line to the picture that corresponds to the ordinal number in the left column.

eighth

third

sixth

ninth

seventh

second

fourth

first

fifth

tenth

Get in Line!

Directions: These children are waiting to see a movie. Look at them and follow the directions.

1. Color the person who is **first** in line yellow.

2. Color the person who is **last** in line **blue**.

3. Color the person who is **second** in line **pink**.

4. Circle the person who is at the **end** of the line.

Add It Up: 1–2

Addition means "putting together" or adding two or more numbers to find the sum. "+" is a plus sign. It means to add the 2 numbers. "=" is an equals sign. It tells how much they are together.

Directions: Count the cats and tell how many.

Add It Up: 3–6

Directions: Practice writing the numbers and then add. Draw dots to help, if needed.

3 _____

4 _____

5 _____

6 _____

$$2$$
$$+4$$
——

$$1$$
$$+4$$
——

$$3$$
$$+2$$
——

$$1$$
$$+2$$
——

Add It Up: 6–8

Directions: Practice writing the numbers and then add.
Draw dots to help, if needed.

6 _____

7 _____

8 _____

$$\begin{array}{r} 3 \\ +4 \\ \hline \end{array}$$

$$\begin{array}{r} 5 \\ +1 \\ \hline \end{array}$$

$$\begin{array}{r} 2 \\ +6 \\ \hline \end{array}$$

$$\begin{array}{r} 4 \\ +4 \\ \hline \end{array}$$

Add It Up: 7–9

Directions: Practice writing the numbers and then add.
Draw dots to help, if needed.

7 _____

8 _____

9 _____

$$\begin{array}{r} 8 \\ +1 \\ \hline \end{array}$$

$$\begin{array}{r} 3 \\ +5 \\ \hline \end{array}$$

$$\begin{array}{r} 2 \\ +7 \\ \hline \end{array}$$

$$\begin{array}{r} 6 \\ +1 \\ \hline \end{array}$$

Add It Up!

Directions: Draw the correct number of dots next to the numbers in each problem. Add up the number of dots to find your answer.

Example:

$$3$$
$$\underline{+2}$$

• • •
• •

$$2 + 2 = \underline{\qquad}$$

• • • •

$$4$$
$$\underline{+2}$$

$$1 + 5 = \underline{\qquad}$$

$$3$$
$$\underline{+1}$$

$$4 + 3 = \underline{\qquad}$$

$$6$$
$$\underline{+2}$$

$$5 + 3 = \underline{\qquad}$$

Tool Time

Directions: Count the tools in each tool box. Write your answers in the blanks. Circle the problem that matches your answer.

4

$$\begin{array}{r} 2 \\ +2 \\ \hline \end{array}$$ (circled)
$$\begin{array}{r} 2 \\ +1 \\ \hline 3 \end{array}$$

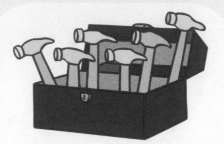

6

$$\begin{array}{r} 5 \\ +0 \\ \hline 5 \end{array}$$
$$\begin{array}{r} 4 \\ +2 \\ \hline 6 \end{array}$$

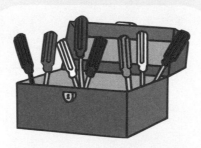

___

$$\begin{array}{r} 6 \\ +2 \\ \hline \end{array}$$
$$\begin{array}{r} 4 \\ +3 \\ \hline \end{array}$$

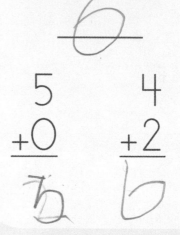

___

$$\begin{array}{r} 3 \\ +1 \\ \hline \end{array}$$
$$\begin{array}{r} 2 \\ +3 \\ \hline \end{array}$$

In the Doghouse

Directions: Add the numbers. Put your answers in the doghouses.

Example: 4 + 2 =  6

2 + 6 =

7 + 3 =

6 + 1 =

4 + 5 =

6 + 2 =

7 + 2 =

Subtraction Action: 1–3

Subtraction means "taking away" or subtracting one number from another. "–" is a minus sign. It means to subtract the second number from the first.

Directions: Practice writing the numbers and then subtract. Draw dots and cross them out, if needed.

1

2

3

$$3 \\ -1 \\ \overline{2}$$

$$4 \\ -3 \\ \overline{}$$

$$2 \\ -1 \\ \overline{}$$

$$3 \\ -2 \\ \overline{}$$

Subtraction Action: 3–6

Directions: Practice writing the numbers and then subtract. Draw dots and cross them out, if needed.

3

4

5

6

$$\begin{array}{r} 5 \\ -2 \\ \hline \end{array}$$

$$\begin{array}{r} 6 \\ -1 \\ \hline \end{array}$$

$$\begin{array}{r} 6 \\ -3 \\ \hline \end{array}$$

$$\begin{array}{r} 5 \\ -1 \\ \hline \end{array}$$

Fresh and Fruity

Directions: Count the fruit in each bowl. Write your answers in the blanks. Circle the problem that matches your answer.

4
———

⑤   4
-1   -2

———

3   4
-0   -2

———

5   4
-1   -3

———

3   5
-2   -0

Flower Power

Directions: Count the flowers. Write your answers in the blanks. Circle the problem that matches your answer.

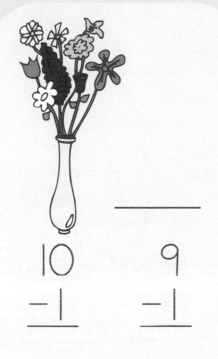

_____

10	9
-1	-1

_____

7	9
-2	-3

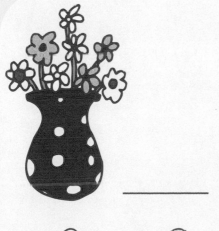

_____

9	8
-6	-0

_____

10	8
-2	-1

Solve It!

Directions: Solve the problems. Remember, addition means "putting together" or adding two or more numbers to find the sum. Subtraction means "taking away" or subtracting one number from another.

1 + 3 = ___   4 − 3 = ___   4 + 5 = ___

6 + 1 = ___   7 − 2 = ___   8 − 4 = ___

9 − 1 = ___   10 − 3 = ___

5 − 2 = ___   6 + 3 = ___

8 + 2 = ___   5 + 5 = ___

Patchwork Math

Remember, addition means "putting together" or adding two or more numbers to find the sum. Subtraction means "taking away" or subtracting one number from another.

Directions: Solve the problems. From your answers, use the code to color the quilt.

Color:

6's blue

7's yellow

8's green

9's red

10's orange

$$6 + 3$$

$$12 - 6 =$$

$$10 - 2 =$$

$$9 + 1$$

$$10 - 4$$

$$4 + 6$$

$$11 - 2$$

$$5 + 5$$

$$12 - 6$$

$$10 - 1$$

$$3 + 4$$

$$12 - 5$$

$$10 - 3$$

$$6 + 1$$

$$11 - 5$$

$$3 + 5$$

$$11 - 1$$

$$4 + 4$$

$$6 + 2$$

$$6 + 3$$

$$1 + 5 =$$

$$9 - 2 =$$

$$6 + 2 =$$

Review

Directions: Trace the numbers. Work the problems

$$\begin{array}{r} 9 \\ -3 \\ \hline \end{array}$$

$$\begin{array}{r} 6 \\ +2 \\ \hline \end{array}$$

$$\begin{array}{r} 3 \\ +4 \\ \hline \end{array}$$

$$\begin{array}{r} 5 \\ +4 \\ \hline \end{array}$$

$$\begin{array}{r} 9 \\ -5 \\ \hline \end{array}$$

$$\begin{array}{r} 7 \\ +2 \\ \hline \end{array}$$

$$\begin{array}{r} 4 \\ -2 \\ \hline \end{array}$$

$$\begin{array}{r} 6 \\ +3 \\ \hline \end{array}$$

$$\begin{array}{r} 9 \\ -7 \\ \hline \end{array}$$

Get to Know Zero

Directions: Write the number.

Example:

How many monkeys?

_3_

How many monkeys?

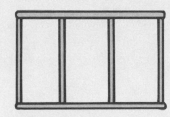

_0_

How many kites?

_____

How many kites?

_____

How many flowers?

_____

How many flowers?

_____

How many apples?

_____

How many apples?

_____

Picture This: Addition

Directions: Solve the number problem under each picture.

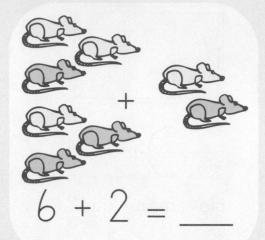

$6 + 2 =$ ___

$3 + 1 =$ ___

$5 + 3 =$ ___

$1 + 7 =$ ___

$4 + 5 =$ ___

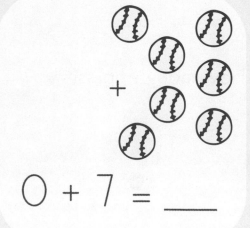

$0 + 7 =$ ___

Picture This: Addition

Directions: Solve the number problem under each picture.

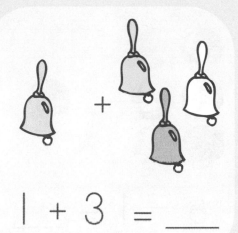

1 + 3 = ___

2 + 4 = ___

3 + 5 = ___

6 + 2 = ___

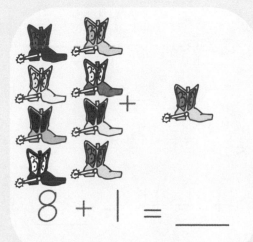

8 + 1 = ___

0 + 7 = ___

Picture This: Subtraction

Directions: Solve the number problem under each picture.

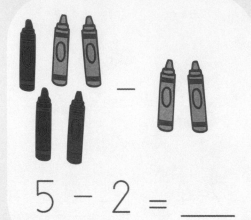

5 − 2 = ___

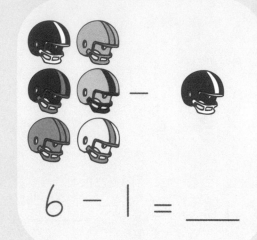

6 − 1 = ___

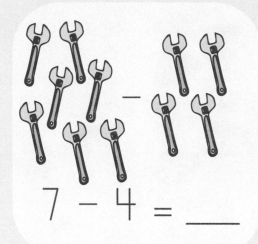

7 − 4 = ___

8 − 3 = ___

9 − 2 = ___

4 − 4 = ___

Picture This: Subtraction

Directions: Solve the number problem under each picture.

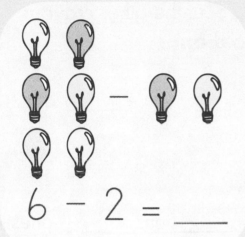

6 − 2 = ___

9 − 5 = ___

8 − 2 = ___

4 − 1 = ___

8 − 1 = ___

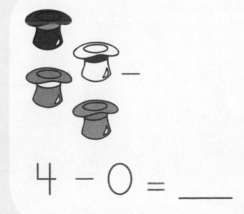

4 − 0 = ___

Know Your Place

The place value of a digit, or numeral, is shown by where it is in the number. For example, in the number **23**, **2** has the place value of **tens**, and **3** is **ones**.

Directions: Count the groups of ten crayons and write the number by the word **tens**. Count the other crayons and write the number by the word **ones**.

Example: [crayons] + [crayon] = __1__ ten + __1__ one

[two bundles] + [two crayons] = _____ tens + _____ ones

[four bundles] + [one bundle] = _____ tens + _____ ones

[six bundles] + [one crayon] = _____ tens + _____ ones

6 tens + 3 ones = _____   5 tens + 1 one = _____

3 tens + 8 ones = _____   9 tens + 7 ones = _____

4 tens + 5 ones = _____   2 tens + 8 ones = _____

Know Your Place

Directions: Write the answers in the correct spaces.

 **tens ones**

3 tens, 2 ones   ____ ____ = ____

3 tens, 7 ones   ____ ____ = ____

9 tens, 1 one   ____ ____ = ____

5 tens, 6 ones   ____ ____ = ____

6 tens, 5 ones   ____ ____ = ____

6 tens, 8 ones   ____ ____ = ____

2 tens, 8 ones   ____ ____ = ____

4 tens, 9 ones   ____ ____ = ____

1 ten, 4 ones   ____ ____ = ____

8 tens, 2 ones   ____ ____ = ____

4 tens, 2 ones   ____ ____ = ____

28 =   ____ tens, ____ ones

64 =   ____ tens, ____ ones

56 =   ____ tens, ____ ones

72 =   ____ tens, ____ ones

38 =   ____ tens, ____ ones

17 =   ____ ten, ____ ones

63 =   ____ tens, ____ ones

12 =   ____ ten, ____ ones

On a Ride with Five

Directions: Count by fives to draw a path to the playground.

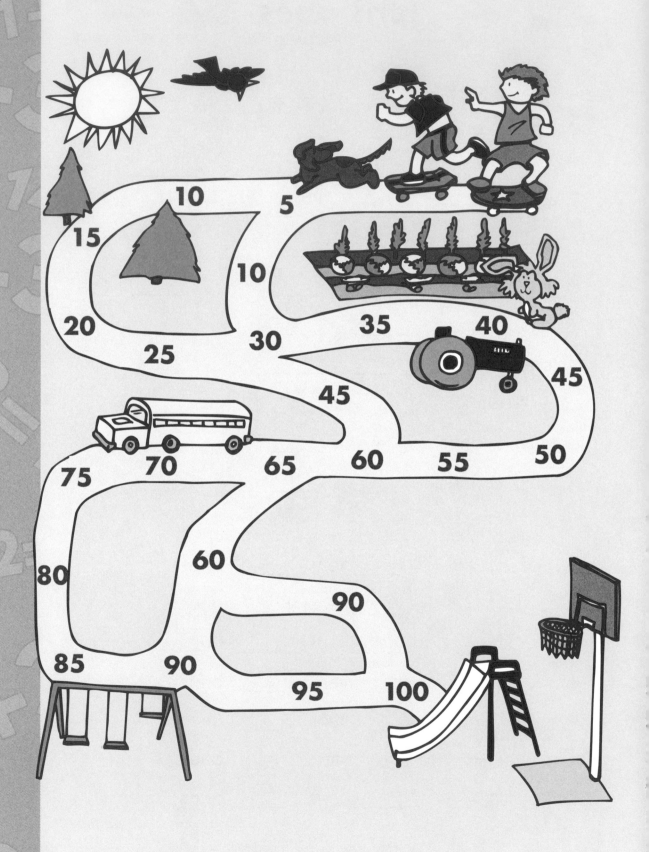

On the Trail of Tens

Directions: Count in order by tens to draw the path the boy takes to the store.

Counting on Crayons

Directions: Circle groups of ten crayons. Add the remaining ones to make the correct number.

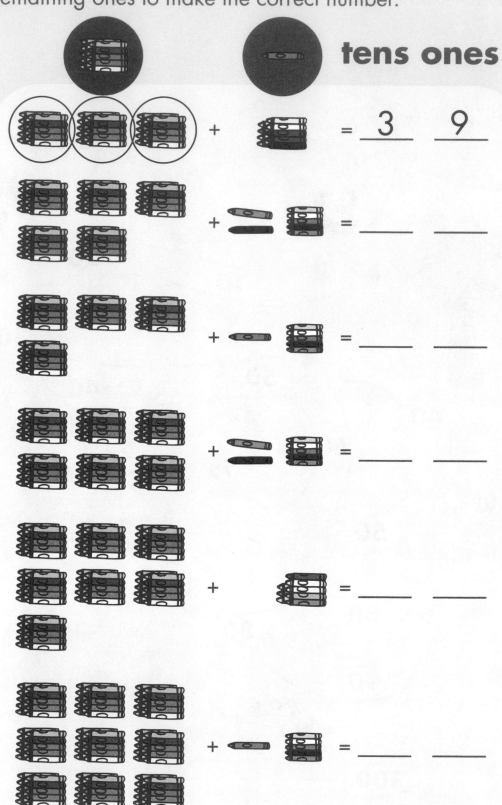

tens ones

= __3__ __9__

6 + 6 = ___   8 + 4 = ___   9 + 5 = ___

Crayon Cross-out

Directions: Count the crayons in each group. Put an **X** through the number of crayons being subtracted. How many are left?

— 5 = <u>10</u>

— 4 = ___

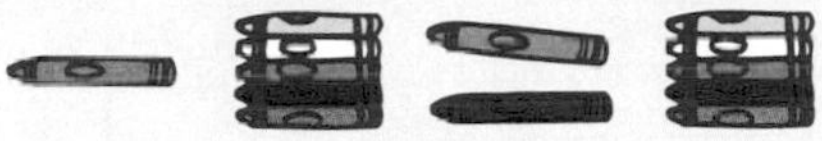

— 7 = ___

— 6 = ___

— 5 = ___

— 8 = ___

13 – 8 = ___   11 – 5 = ___   12 – 9 = ___

14 – 7 = ___   10 – 7 = ___   13 – 3 = ___

15 – 9 = ___   11 – 8 = ___   12 – 10 = ___

Fair and Square

A square is a figure with four corners and four sides of the same length. This is a square ☐.

Directions: Find the squares and circle them.

Directions: Trace the word. Write the word.

Circles All Around

A circle is a figure that is round. This is a circle ◯.

Directions: Find the circles and put a square around them.

Directions: Trace the word. Write the word.

circle

Totally Triangles

A triangle is a figure with three corners and three sides. This is a triangle △ .

Directions: Find the triangles and put a circle around them.

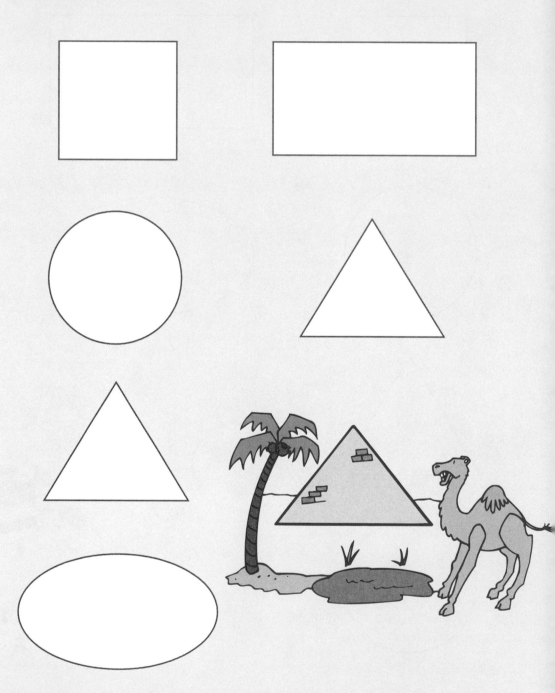

Directions: Trace the word. Write the word.

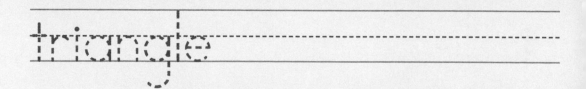

triangle

Make Room for Rectangles

A rectangle is a figure four corners and four sides. Sides opposite each other are the same length. This is a rectangle ▭.

Directions: Find the rectangles and put a circle around them.

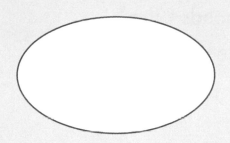

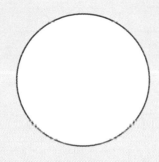

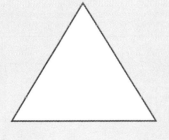

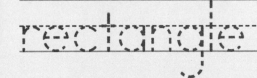

Directions: Trace the word. Write the word.

rectangle

Ovals and Diamonds

An oval is an egg-shaped figure. A diamond is a figure with four sides of the same length. It's corners form points at the top, sides and bottom. This is an oval ⬭. This is a diamond ◇.

Directions: Color the ovals **red**. Color the diamonds **blue**.

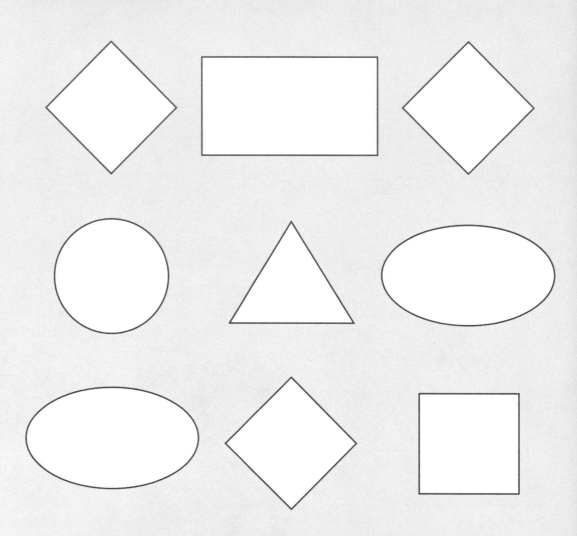

Directions: Trace the word. Write the word.

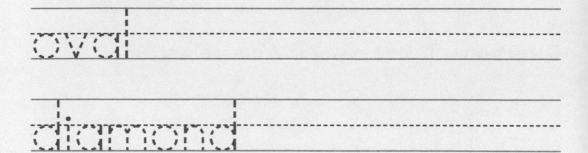

Review

Directions: Color the shapes in the picture as shown.

black **red**  orange yellow **blue** green

Review

Directions: Trace the circles **red**.

Trace the squares **blue**.

Trace the rectangles yellow.

Trace the triangles green.

Trace the ovals **purple**.

Trace the diamonds orange.

Shape Up

Directions: Look at the shapes. Answer the questions.

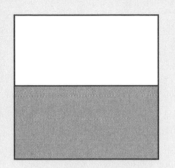  

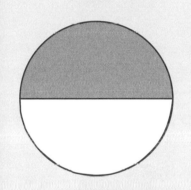 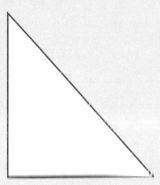 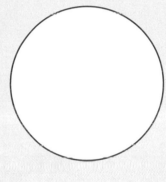

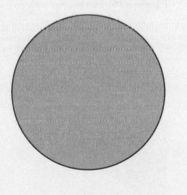  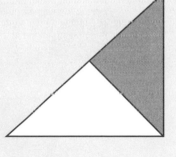

1. How many all-white shapes? _____

2. How many all-blue shapes? _____

3. How many half-white shapes? _____

4. How many all-blue stars? _____

5. How many all-white circles? _____

6. How many half-blue shapes? _____

Ship Shape

Directions: Draw an **X** on the shapes in each row that do not match the first shape.

Pattern Play

Directions: Draw a line from the box on the left to the box on the right with the same shape and color pattern.

  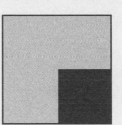 

 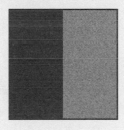 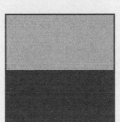 

Pattern Play

Directions: Circle the shape in the middle box that matches the one on the left. Draw another shape with the same pattern in the box on the right.

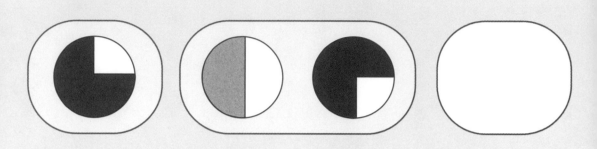

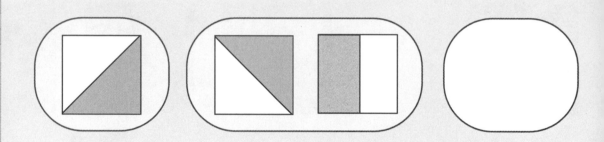

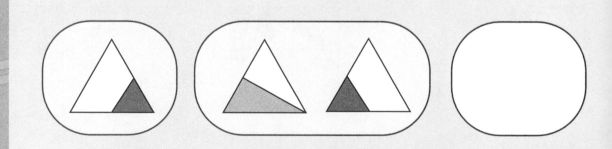

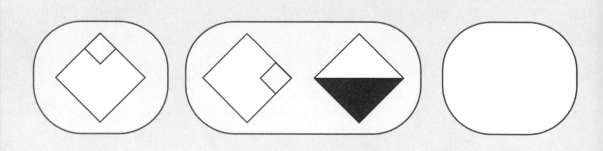

Pattern Play

Directions: Fill in the missing shape in each row. Then, color it.

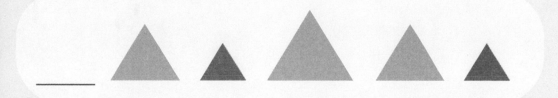

Fraction Action: Whole and Half

A fraction is a number that names part of a whole, such as $\frac{1}{2}$ or $\frac{3}{4}$.

Directions: Color half of each object.

Example:

$\frac{1}{2}$

Whole apple   **Half an apple**

 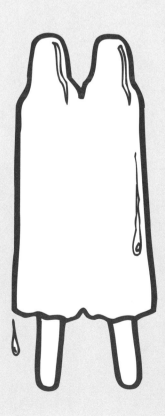

Fraction Action: Halves $\frac{1}{2}$

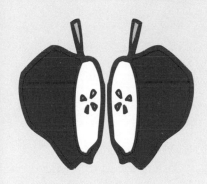

$\frac{1}{2}$ Part shaded or divided
   Number of equal parts.

Directions: Color only the shapes that show halves.

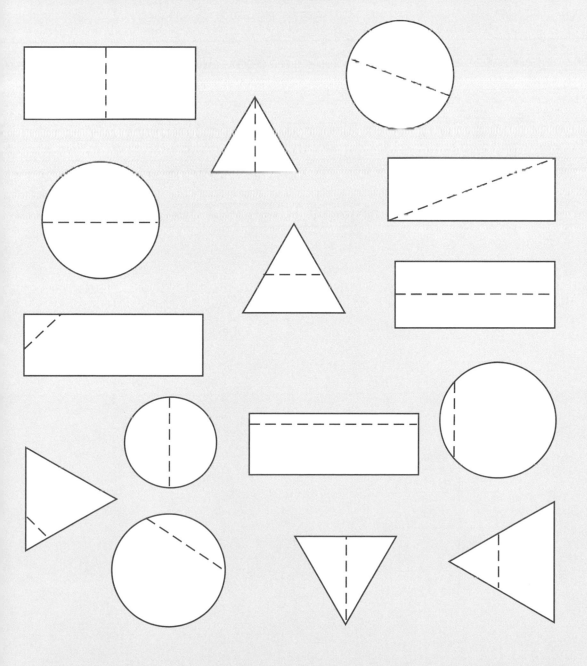

Fraction Action:
Thirds and Fourths

Directions: Each object has 3 equal parts.
Color one section.

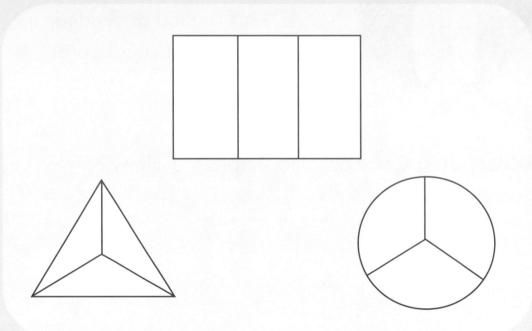

Directions: Each object has 4 equal parts.
Color one section.

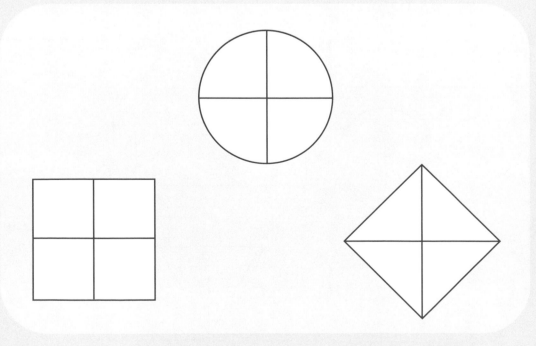

Review

Directions: Count the equal parts, then write the fraction.

Example:

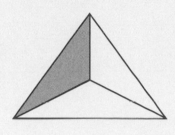

Shaded part = $\underline{\hspace{0.3em}1\hspace{0.3em}}$

Equal parts = $\underline{\hspace{0.3em}3\hspace{0.3em}}$

Write $\dfrac{1}{3}$

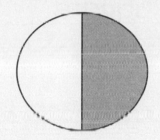

Shaded part = $\underline{\hspace{0.3em}1\hspace{0.3em}}$

Equal parts = $\underline{\hspace{1.5em}}$

Write $\underline{\hspace{1.5em}}$

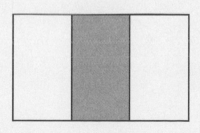

Shaded part = $\underline{\hspace{0.3em}1\hspace{0.3em}}$

Equal parts = $\underline{\hspace{1.5em}}$

Write $\underline{\hspace{1.5em}}$

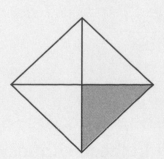

Shaded part = $\underline{\hspace{0.3em}1\hspace{0.3em}}$

Equal parts = $\underline{\hspace{1.5em}}$

Write $\underline{\hspace{1.5em}}$

On the Right Track

Directions: Draw a straight line from A to B. Use a different color crayon for each line.

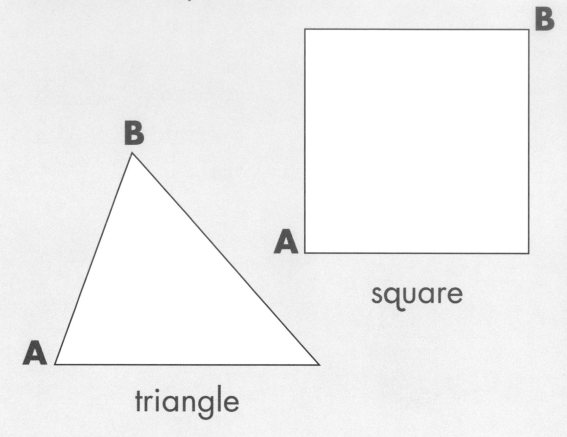

square

triangle

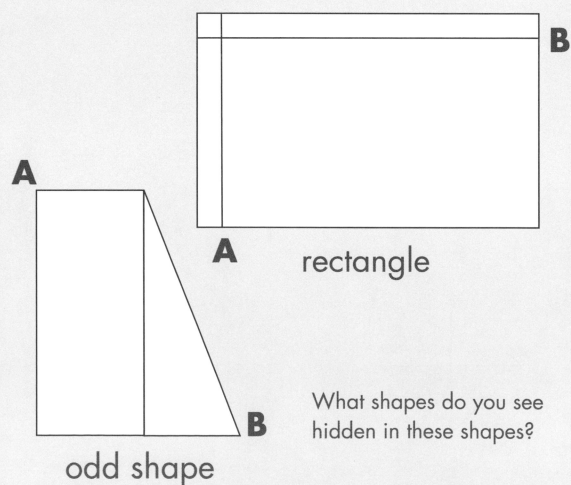

rectangle

odd shape

What shapes do you see hidden in these shapes?

Finding a Friend

Help Megan find Mark.

Directions: Trace a path from Megan to Mark.

How many different paths
can she follow to reach him? _____

On the Honey Trail

Directions: Use different colors to trace three paths the bear could take to get the honey.

Right on Time!

The short hand of the clock tells the hour. The long hand tells how many minutes after the hour. When the minute hand is on the **12**, it is the beginning of the hour.

Directions: Look at each clock. Write the time.

Example:

_____ **3** _____ o'clock

 _____ o'clock

 _____ o'clock

 _____ o'clock

 _____ o'clock

 _____ o'clock

 _____ o'clock

It's About Time

The short hand of the clock tells the hour. The long hand tells how many minutes after the hour. When the minute hand is on the **6**, it is on the half-hour. A half-hour is thirty minutes. It is written **:30**, such as **5:30**.

Directions: Look at each clock. Write the time.

Example:

hour   half-hour

__1__ : __30__

___ : ___   ___ : ___

___ : ___   ___ : ___

___ : ___   ___ : ___

Rock Around the Clock

Directions: Fill in the numbers on the clock face. Count by fives around the clock.

There are 60 minutes in one hour.

Time to Match

Directions: Match the time on the clock with the digital time.

10:00

5:00

3:00

9:00

2:00

Review

Directions: Look at the time on the digital clocks and draw the hands on the clocks.

Directions: Look at each clock. Write the time.

 _____ o'clock  _____ o'clock

Directions: Look at each clock. Write the time.

_____ : _____   _____ : _____   _____ : _____

204 MATH

Money Sense

A penny is worth one cent. It is written **1¢** or **$.01**. A nickel is worth five cents. It is written **5¢** or **$.05**. A dime is worth ten cents. It is written **10¢** or **$.10**.

Directions: Add the coins pictured and write the total amounts in the blanks.

Example:

dime   **nickel**   **nickel**   **pennies**

10¢ = 5¢ + 5¢ =   10¢

10¢   +   1¢   = _____¢

10¢   +   _____¢   = _____¢

_____¢ + _____¢ + _____¢ = _____¢

_____¢   +   _____¢   = _____¢

How Much?

Directions: Match the amounts in each purse to the price tags.

Review

Directions: What time is it?

_____ o'clock

Directions: Draw the hands on each clock.

2:30   7:30

11:00

Directions: How much money?

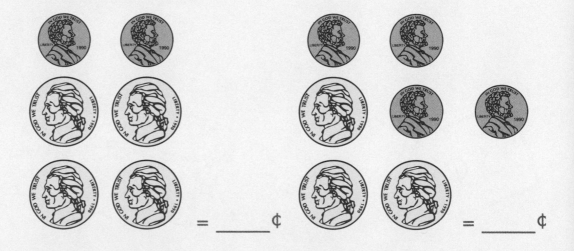

= _____ ¢   = _____ ¢

Directions: Add or subtract.

9 + 3 = _____   6 + 8 = _____   15 − 9 = _____

12 − 8 = _____   12 + 2 = _____   7 + 6 = _____

Inch by Inch

A ruler has 12 inches. 12 inches equal 1 foot.

Directions: Cut out the ruler at the bottom of the page. Measure the objects to the nearest inch.

The screwdriver is _____ inches long.

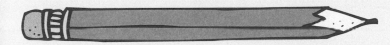

The pencil is _____ inches long.

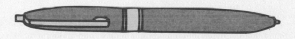

The pen is _____ inches long.

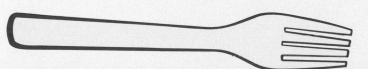

The fork is _____ inches long.

Cut ✂ ---

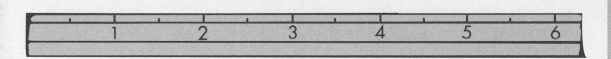

This page is blank for the cutting activity
on the opposite side.

Abbreviation: A short way of writing words. **Examples:** Mon., Tues., etc.

Addition: "Putting together" or adding two or more numbers to find the sum.

Alphabetical (ABC) Order: Putting letters or words in the order in which they appear in the alphabet.

Antonyms: Words that are opposites. **Example:** big and small are opposites.

Asking Sentences: Sentences that ask a question. An asking sentence begins with a capital letter and ends with a question mark.

Beginning Consonants: Consonant sounds that come at the beginning of words.

Beginning Sounds: The sounds you hear first in a word.

Capital Letters: Letters that are used at the beginning of names of people, places, days, months and holidays. Capital letters are also used at the beginning of sentences. These letters (A, B, C, D, E, F, G, H, I, J, K, L, M, N, O, P, Q, R, S, T, U, V, W, X, Y and Z) are sometimes called uppercase or "big" letters.

Circle: A figure that is round. It looks like this: ◯

Classifying: Putting objects, words or ideas that are alike into categories.

Compound Words: Two words that are put together to make one new word. **Example:** house + boat = houseboat.

Comprehension: Understanding what is seen, heard or read.

Consonant Blends: Two consonant sounds put together.

Consonants: The letters b, c, d, f, g, h, j, k, l, m, n, p, q, r, s, t, v, w, x, y and z. Consonants are all the letters except a, e, i, o and u.

Describing Words: Words that tell more about a person, place or thing.

Diamond: A figure with four sides of the same length. Its corners form points at the top, sides and bottom. It looks like this: ◇

Digits: The symbols used to write numbers: 0, 1, 2, 3, 4, 5, 6, 7, 8 and 9.

Dime: Ten cents. It is written 10¢ or $.10.

Directions: Doing what the instructions say to do.

Ending Consonants: Consonant sounds which come at the end of words.

Ending Sounds: The sounds made by the last letters of words.

Following Directions: Doing what the directions say to do.

Fraction: A number that names part of a whole, such as $\frac{1}{2}$ or $\frac{2}{3}$.

Half-Hour: Thirty minutes. When the long hand of the clock is pointing to the six, the time is on the half-hour. It is written :30, such as 5:30.

Homophones: Words that sound the same but are spelled differently and mean different things. **Example:** blue and blew.

Hour: Sixty minutes. The short hand of a clock tells the hour. It is written 2:00.

Long Vowels: The letters a, e, i, o and u which say the "long" or letter name sound. Long a is the sound you hear in hay. Long e is the sound you hear in me. Long i is the sound you hear in pie. Long o is the sound you hear in no. Long u is the sound you hear in cute.

Making Inferences: Using logic to figure out what is unspoken but known to be true.

Nickel: Five cents. It is written 5¢ or $.05.

Nouns: Name a person, place or thing.

Opposites: Things that are different in every way.

Ordinal Numbers: Numbers that indicate order in a series, such as first, second or third.

Oval: A figure that is egg-shaped. It looks like this: ◯

Pattern: A repeated arrangement of pictures, letters or shapes.

Penny: One cent. It is written 1¢ or $.01.

Period: Tells you when to stop reading and is found at the end of sentences. It looks like this: .

Picture Clues: Looking at the pictures to figure out meaning.

Place Value: The value of a digit, or numeral, shown by where it is in the number. For example, in the number 23, 2 has the place value of tens and 3 is ones.

Predicting: Telling what is likely to happen based on available facts.

Rectangle: A figure with four corners and four sides. Sides opposite each other are the same length. It looks like this: ▭

Rhymes: Words with the same ending sounds.

Rhyming Words: Words that sound alike at the end of the word. **Example:** cat and rat.

Same and Different: Being able to tell how things are alike and not alike.

Sentence: A group of words that tells a complete idea.

Sequencing: Putting numbers in the correct order, such as 7, 8, 9.

Short Vowels: The letters a, e, i, o and u which say the short sound. Short a is the sound you hear in ant. Short e is the sound you hear in elephant. Short i is the sound you hear in igloo. Short o is the sound you hear in octopus. Short u is the sound you hear in umbrella.

Similar: Things that are almost the same.

Square: A figure with four corners and four sides of the same length. It looks like this: ☐

Subtraction: "Taking away" or subtracting one number from another. For example: $10 - 3 = 7$.

Super Silent E: The e that is added to some words which changes the short vowel sound to a long vowel sound. **Example:** rip + e = ripe.

Synonyms: Words that mean the same thing. **Example:** small and little.

Telling Sentences: Sentences that tell something. A telling sentence begins with a capital letter and ends with a period.

Tracking: Following a path.

Triangle: A figure with three corners and three sides. It looks like this: △

Verbs: Words that tell what a person or thing can do.

Vowels: The letters a, e, i, o, u and sometimes y.

Addition

Make your own "plus" sign. Glue two toothpicks or popsicle sticks together. Then, your child can create groups of objects on either side of the "plus" sign to add.

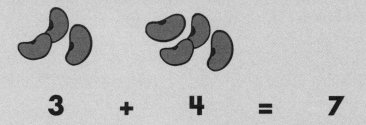

4   +   1   =   5

Use dry beans or other small objects to practice counting. Have your child divide ten beans into two separate groups and combine them by adding. Have your child write the number problem on paper and read it to you.

3   +   4   =   7

Look through magazines with your child. Encourage him/her to create addition problems from the pictures. For example: "One Mommy plus two children equals three!"

Alphabetical (ABC) Order

Write three or four words (names of family members, color words, objects found in the kitchen) on a sheet of paper. Space them so they can be cut out and rearranged in random order. Have your child move them around so that they are in the correct order. At first, you will need to be careful not to include two words that begin with the same letter. As your child masters ABC order, however, you can show him/her how to use the second letter of a word when doing alphabetical order. Words such as "brown" and "blue" both begin with the letter "b," so your child would need to look at the "r" and the "l" to help him/her determine which word would come first.

Give your child a copy of your weekly grocery list, and let him/her rewrite it for you in alphabetical order.

Show your child a dictionary. Lead him/her to discover that the words are listed in alphabetical order. Purchase an inexpensive picture dictionary for your child to use in his/her writing, and encourage him/her to "look up" words he/she wants to spell correctly.

Classifying

Classifying involves putting objects, words or ideas that are alike into categories. Objects can be classified in more than one way. For example, hats could be sorted by size, color or season worn. If your child creates a category you had not considered, praise him/her for thinking creatively.

Your child could sort the clothing in his/her closet. He/she could sort it according to the season each item is worn, by color, type of clothing or even likes and dislikes. You can also have your child help you sort laundry.

At the grocery store, talk about the layout of the store and how items are arranged. For example, fruits are together, vegetables are together, cooking supplies are together, soups are together, etc. Talk about why items would be arranged in groups like that. What would happen if they were not arranged in groups? Have your child help you find what you need by having him/her decide what section of the store it would be in. After finding the item, talk about alternate places the item could be found.

When planning a family vacation, collect travel brochures on possible destinations and sites to see. Have your child classify the brochures according to location, activity or places you may or may not want to visit. Use these groupings to plan your trip.

Recycling is a good way to practice classifying. Label recycling containers clearly (paper, plastic, glass, metal). Your child's job can be to sort the recyclables and put them in the correct containers.

Let your child help you organize the kitchen cupboards, a closet or dresser drawer. Food could be organized into food groups. Clothes and shoes could be sorted by season or color.

Help your child take a poll while riding in the car. Decide on a topic (color of cars, types of vehicles seen, color of houses, etc.). Have your child draw columns on a sheet of paper and label the columns. Each time you or your child spots an object that belongs in a category, have him/her make a tally mark in that column.

Encourage your child to help you as you prepare meals in the kitchen. Talk about the places where kitchen utensils are kept—silverware, glasses, plates, etc. As you dry the dishes or empty the dishwasher, your child can sort the forks, spoons and knives or the plates and glasses. Helping to sort and fold the laundry is another practical way to reinforce this skill.

Arrange an assortment of "like" objects, such as buttons, safety pins, paper clips (all used to fasten things) or chalk, pens, markers (things used to write with), and have your child find something that also belongs in that grouping. You could also arrange an assortment of "like" materials with one object that doesn't belong and have your child remove the wrong one.

Colors

Fill six clear plastic glasses half full with water. Have your child experiment with mixing drops of food coloring into each cup. Talk about the colors created and how they were created. Help your child record his/her findings. For example, red + yellow = orange.

Compound Words

Look for compound words in newspapers and magazines or write compound words on cards, and cut them apart for your child. Challenge your child to match the word parts, glue them together and illustrate them.

Comprehension

Your child can make a poster for a book or movie. Have him/her include the important events, the most exciting parts, his/her favorite part and reasons why someone else should view or read it.

Comprehension involves understanding what is seen, heard or read. To help your child with this skill, talk about a book, picture, movie or television program. Ask your child if he/she likes it and the reasons why or why not. By listening to what he/she says, you can tell whether the book, etc. was understood. If your child does not fully understand part of it, discuss that section further. Reread the book or watch the program again, if possible.

Watch the news with your child and discuss the job of a news reporter. After your child understands what reporters do, create your own newscast. You can be the reporter, and your child can pretend to be a character from a book or movie. Make up the questions together, based on a book he/she has read or a movie he/she has watched. Use the questions for an "interview." If you have a video camera, record your interview, and play it back for your child to watch.

After reading a book, have your child create a book cover for it. The picture should tell about the book and include a brief summary on the back. If the book belongs to your child, he/she could use the cover on the book.

Find a comic strip without words or use a comic strip from the newspaper and cut off the words. Have your child look at the pictures and create words to go along with them. If your child has difficulty writing, you may want to write what he/she says.

Consonants/Vowels

Have your child write the names of family members and graph the number of consonants and vowels in each person's name. Then ask questions to help your child interpret the graph. For example: "Whose name has the most vowels?" "The most consonants?" "Whose name has the most letters?"

Play "Letter Bingo" or "Word Bingo" with your child. Cut pictures from magazines and glue them on a Bingo board. Start by calling out beginning consonant sounds. For example, "Cover words that start with the letter 't.'" You can make the game more difficult by asking your child to identify words by both their beginning and ending sound, as in "Cover the word that begins with a 't' and ends with a 'd.'"

Have your child brainstorm a list of words that have the short a sound (or whatever vowel you're working on) in the beginning or middle. Looking at pictures in books or magazines may help spark ideas.

Counting

Have your child write his/her name. Have him/her count the number of letters in his/her name and the number of times each letter appears. Have your child do the same with your name and other family members' names.

Buy or make a calendar for your child to keep in his/her room. Have your child number the calendar. Put stickers on or draw pictures to mark special days. Have your child cross out each day.

Play the card game "War" with your child. Each player needs an equal number of cards. Explain the value of face cards to your child. Each player places a card facedown and turns it over at the same time. The player with the higher number gets to keep both cards.

Following Directions

Give your child a set of three directions to follow. For example, you could say, "Go to the refrigerator and get a carrot stick. Put it on a small plate. Take it to your father in the garage." You may be able to increase the steps in the sequence, but do not make the skill so difficult that your child gets frustrated. Then, reverse your roles! Have your child give you a set of directions to follow. This change is not only fun for him/her, it is also good practice in giving clear directions.

When playing a new game, read the directions with your child. Then have him/her explain how to play the game. When a friend visits, let your child explain the rules of the game.

Write a note for your child, giving step-by-step directions on how to do something. If he/she cannot read yet, use pictures to show what needs to be done. Encourage your child to follow the directions to complete the task.

Fractions

Let your child help you cut pie or pizza into equal slices.

Peel an orange. Separate the sections and talk about "fractions" as parts of a whole.

Pick clovers. Talk about equal parts as you pull off the petals.

Fold a sheet of paper into four equal sections. Have your child shade three sections blue and one brown. Explain that $\frac{1}{4}$ of the Earth is water and $\frac{1}{4}$ is land.

Letter Sounds

Write each consonant letter on a large index card. Choose four to eight of the cards and lay them out on a table. Say a word that begins with one of the letters and have your child identify the beginning sound. (At first, avoid naming words that begin with blends and digraphs such as frog or shop.) Repeat with other consonant letters.

To help your child develop his/her skill in recognizing beginning and ending sounds, play a game of "I Spy" together. Say, for example, "I see something in this room that starts with the sound of 't,'" or "I spy something that ends with the same sound as 'top.' "Your child should respond with an appropriate object. You can make the game more challenging by using consonant blends, as in "Can you spy something that begins with the same beginning blend as 'glove'?"

Make up letter riddles. **Example:** "I'm thinking of an animal that hops and whose name begins with 'r.' " Have your child guess the answer.

Letter Sounds and ABC Order

Create an ABC scavenger hunt for your child. Provide your child with a list of words and pictures representing each of the 26 letters of the alphabet.
For example:

a   apple

b   ball

c   cat

d   doll

Let him/her collect the items for the scavenger hunt from around your home or neighborhood and label them.

Letter Recognition and Formation

Use glue to "write" the capital and lowercase letters of the alphabet. After the glue dries, encourage your child to trace the letters with his/her fingers. Then encourage him/her to identify the letters with his/her eyes closed!

Using white liquid glue, have your child "write" words in large letters on drawing paper. Then, have your child place thick yarn in the glue to form each letter of the word. When the words dry, your child can trace them with his/her fingers while spelling the words.

On a trip to the beach, encourage your child to write the entire alphabet in the sand before the waves wash the letters away!

Making Inferences

Talk about daily events with your child. Ask your child questions about what he/she thinks might happen next or how a person might have felt about an event. Ask your child how he/she arrived at that answer.

Use questions to encourage your child to think about why people do things. For example, "Why do you think that man is scraping the paint off the house?" "Why do you think we are buying chicken at the store today?" Based upon what your child sees, he/she can come up with information without being told.

Measurement

Purchase a plastic or wooden ruler for your child. Let him/her measure various objects around the house. Record his/her findings and talk about length.

Money

Practice counting by fives with nickels and by tens with dimes.

Let your child label canned goods in your home with "prices." He/she will gain valuable practice counting and exchanging money by playing "store."

Give your child small amounts of money to purchase items when you go shopping. Encourage your child to count his/her change after each transaction.

Encourage your child to create other combinations of money for the same amount. For example, ten cents can be made with one dime, two nickels, ten pennies or one nickel and five pennies.

Number Recognition

Have your child read the numbers on the license plates of other vehicles as you drive around town. This will not only reinforce number recognition but letter recognition as well!

Safety Tip: Make sure your child knows his/her address. Have your child write his/her address (with your assistance) and keep it with him/her:

> My Child
>
> 12345 Oak Street
>
> Any City, Any State   12345

Help your child memorize his/her phone number as well. Have him/her practice writing it and dialing it on the phone.

Number Words

Play hopscotch with your child. Instead of using numbers, write the number words in each hopscotch grid.

Patterns

Patterns can also be made from beads, blocks, paper clips, pencils and any other small objects, either alone or combined (blue block, red block, blue block, red block, . . . pencil, paper clip, paper clip, pencil . . .). Begin a pattern with objects and have your child continue the pattern.

Place Value (Tens and Ones)

Rubber band or glue ten toothpicks together to represent "tens" and let your child practice counting by tens.

Let your child practice "trading" with pennies, dimes and a dollar to reinforce the concept of ones, tens and hundreds. Roll a die and let your child take as many pennies from the "pot" as the die indicates. When he/she has ten pennies, he/she can trade them in for a dime. Continue playing and trading pennies for dimes. When your child gets ten dimes, he/she can trade them in for a dollar!

Predicting

When reading a story to your child, pause often and ask, "What do you think will happen next?" This can also be done with videotapes.

You can also help your child practice predicting by giving clues about where you are going. For example, you might say that you are going to visit someone who lives in a white house. If your child needs more information, give additional clues.

Rhyming Words

Read familiar nursery rhymes to your child, and leave out the last line.
For example:

    Jack and Jill
    Went up the _____ .

Same and Different, Similarities, Opposites

Play a game with your child by giving him/her a clue, such as, "Can you bring me something that looks like a book?" or "Can you find a shirt that is the opposite of white?"

In the car, you can play "I Spy." Take turns with your child finding things that are opposite or similar, then give your child a clue such as, "I spy a sign that is the opposite of go." Have your child guess the object.

Give your child two similar objects such as a baseball and a balloon. Ask him/her to tell you ways the two are alike and ways they are different. Do the same with objects that are not very much alike, such as a ball and a toy truck. Again, ask your child to tell you how they are alike and different.

Sequencing

A daily activity like setting the table can help your child practice sequencing. Develop an order in which objects should be put on the table. You can also have your child put away toys according to size, such as from smallest to largest. Words could be put into alphabetical order.

After reading a story, ask your child to retell the story in his/her own words. Listen to see if he/she orders the events correctly. If not, relate an event in the story and ask your child to tell you what happened next.

Talk to your child about order and sequencing in everyday life. Make lists together.

Example: 1. Go to the bank.
2. Go to the grocery store.

Shapes

Encourage your child to look at the different shapes of traffic signs and road signs. What shapes does your child see?

Shapes are part of our everyday lives. What shapes does your child see in his/her home, yard, etc.? List the shapes and objects. Add more as you find them.

Purchase or make a geoboard. To make a geoboard, pound sixteen 2-inch nails an equal distance apart into a 1-inch thick piece of wood. Pull rubber bands over the nails to create various geometric shapes. Talk with your child about the shapes he/she has created.

When going for a walk, have your child look around for shapes in the environment. For example, the front of a house might be a square, etc. Suggest a shape for your child to find.

Cut a long piece of yarn or string for your child. He/she can use it to make shapes. Draw a shape on a sheet of paper and have your child put the yarn on top of it to trace it. Then, have him/her make the shape without tracing it first. Do this with other shapes.

Spelling

Purchase magnetic alphabet letters and let your child practice spelling words and reading them to you. You can spell a word for your child, leaving out the vowel, as in "c _ t." Have your child add a vowel to complete the word.

Have your child write words on an index card with a black marker. Using a different colored crayon or marker to write the word again, have him/her "shadow" the first spelling. Let your child repeat this using several colors to create a "rainbow" effect.

Have your child spell words with alphabet soup letters, alphabet cereal letters or alphabet pasta letters.

Let your child spell words with bread dough letters. To make bread dough, help your child mix together the ingredients listed below.

$3\frac{3}{4}$ cups whole wheat flour

2 cups buttermilk
$\frac{1}{4}$ cup wheat germ

2 teaspoons baking soda
1 cup molasses

1 cup raisins

On wax paper, have your child roll out each piece of dough like a snake. Then, help him/her form each piece into a letter of the alphabet. Place the letters on a greased cookie sheet and bake at 350 degrees for 20 minutes or until golden brown.

Story Order

Encourage your child to tell you about his/her day. Write each event of your child's day on a separate strip of paper as he/she relates them to you. Then, cut the strips apart, and challenge him/her to rearrange the events in the correct order.

Tracking

To practice tracking, your child can make a road out of blocks, cardboard or paper. Then, he/she can "drive" a toy car on the road.

If your child has a bike or tricycle, you can set up a course for him/her to follow. This could also be done on in-line skates or a skateboard. He/she can practice tracking by following a jogging path. Mazes also provide practice in tracking. Provide a city map or draw one of your own. Point out where you are and where you are going. Let your child help find the shortest route to follow.

Writing

Fold a sheet of construction paper into a large cube-shaped block. Before folding, write a word on each side of the cube. Have your child throw the block, read the word that is faceup and write a sentence using the word.

10 Letter to Letter

Directions: In each set, match the lowercase letter to the uppercase letter.

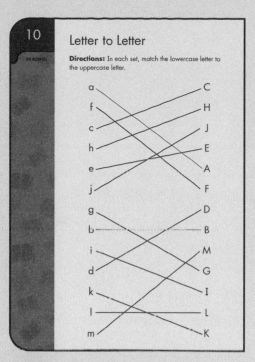

11 Letter to Letter

Directions: In each set, match the lowercase letter to the uppercase letter.

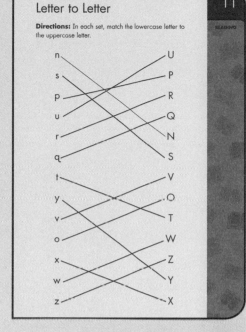

12 Consonant Roundup: B, C, D, F

Beginning consonants are the sounds that come at the beginning of words. Consonants are the letters b, c, d, f, g, h, j, k, l, m, n, p, q, r, s, t, v, w, x, y and z.

Directions: Say the name of each letter. Say the sound each letter makes. Circle the letters that make the **beginning** sound for each picture.

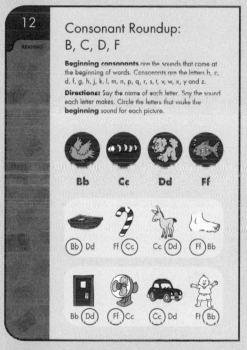

13 Consonant Roundup: G, H, J, K

Directions: Say the name of each letter. Say the sound each letter makes. Draw a line from each letter pair to the picture which begins with that sound.

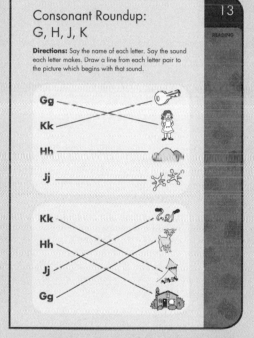

14 Consonant Roundup: L, M, N, P

Directions: Say the name of each letter. Say the sound each letter makes. Trace the letter pair that makes the beginning sound in each picture.

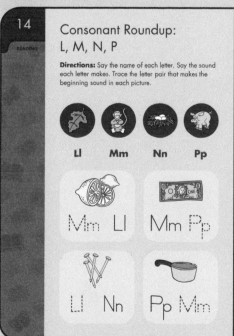

15 Consonant Roundup: Q, R, S, T

Directions: Say the name of each letter. Say the sound each letter makes. Draw a line from each letter pair to the picture which begins with that sound.

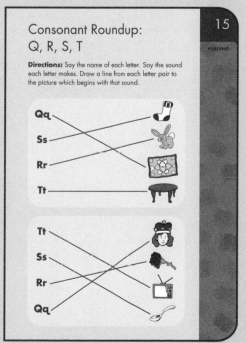

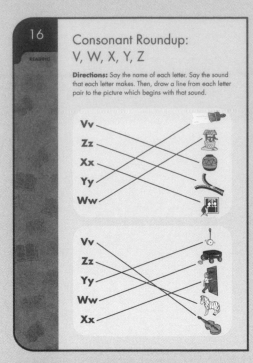

16

Consonant Roundup:
V, W, X, Y, Z

Directions: Say the name of each letter. Say the sound that each letter makes. Then, draw a line from each letter pair to the picture which begins with that sound.

Vv
Zz
Xx
Yy
Ww

Vv
Zz
Yy
Ww
Xx

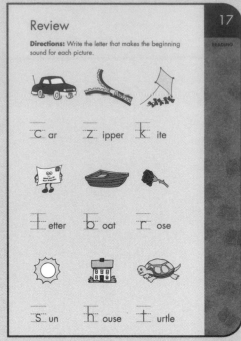

17

Review

Directions: Write the letter that makes the beginning sound for each picture.

C ar   Z ipper   K ite

L etter   b oat   r ose

S un   h ouse   t urtle

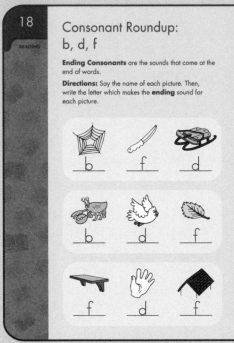

18

Consonant Roundup:
b, d, f

Ending Consonants are the sounds that come at the end of words.

Directions: Say the name of each picture. Then, write the letter which makes the **ending** sound for each picture.

b   f   d

b   d   f

f   d   f

19

Consonant Roundup:
k, l, p

Directions: Trace the letters in each row. Say the name of each picture. Then, color the pictures in each row which end with that sound.

k

l

p

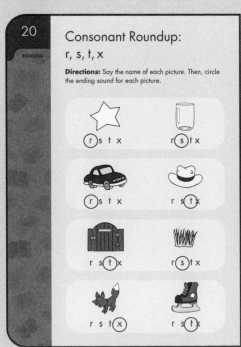

20

Consonant Roundup:
r, s, t, x

Directions: Say the name of each picture. Then, circle the ending sound for each picture.

(r) s t x   r (s) t x

(r) s t x   r s (t) x

r s (t) x   r (s) t x

r s t (x)   r s (t) x

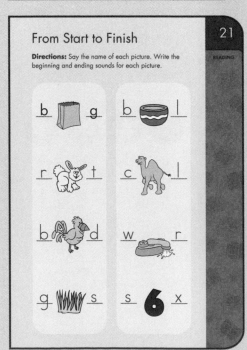

21

From Start to Finish

Directions: Say the name of each picture. Write the beginning and ending sounds for each picture.

b ___ g   b ___ l

r ___ t   c ___ l

b ___ d   w ___ r

g ___ s   s ___ x

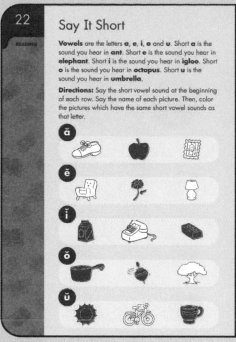

22 Say It Short

Vowels are the letters **a**, **e**, **i**, **o** and **u**. Short **a** is the sound you hear in **ant**. Short **e** is the sound you hear in **elephant**. Short **i** is the sound you hear in **igloo**. Short **o** is the sound you hear in **octopus**. Short **u** is the sound you hear in **umbrella**.

Directions: Say the short vowel sound at the beginning of each row. Say the name of each picture. Then, color the pictures which have the same short vowel sounds as that letter.

ă
ĕ
ĭ
ŏ
ŭ

23 Say It Short

Directions: In each box are three pictures. The words that name the pictures have missing letters. Write **a, e, i, o** or **u** to finish the words.

p_e_n   b_u_g

p_i_n   b_a_g

p_a_n   b_e_g

c_a_t   h_i_t

c_o_t   h_a_t

c_u_t   h_o_t

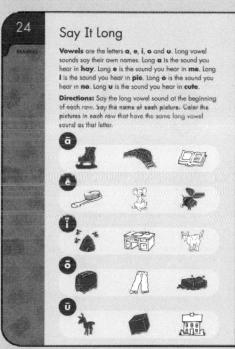

24 Say It Long

Vowels are the letters **a**, **e**, **i**, **o** and **u**. Long vowel sounds say their own names. Long **a** is the sound you hear in **hay**. Long **e** is the sound you hear in **me**. Long **i** is the sound you hear in **pie**. Long **o** is the sound you hear in **no**. Long **u** is the sound you hear in **cute**.

Directions: Say the long vowel sound at the beginning of each row. Say the name of each picture. Color the pictures in each row that have the same long vowel sound as that letter.

ā
ē
ī
ō
ū

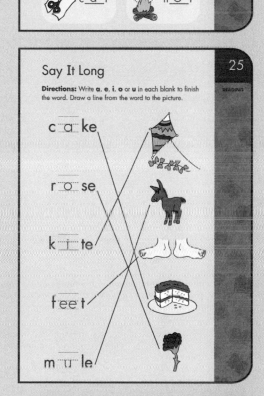

25 Say It Long

Directions: Write **a**, **e**, **i**, **o** or **u** in each blank to finish the word. Draw a line from the word to the picture.

c_a_ke

r_o_se

k_i_te

f_ee_t

m_u_le

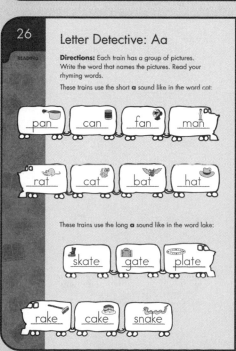

26 Letter Detective: Aa

Directions: Each train has a group of pictures. Write the word that names the pictures. Read your rhyming words.

These trains use the short **a** sound like in the word cat:

pan   can   fan   man

rat   cat   bat   hat

These trains use the long **a** sound like in the word lake:

skate   gate   plate

rake   cake   snake

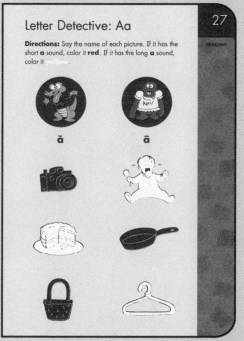

27 Letter Detective: Aa

Directions: Say the name of each picture. If it has the short **a** sound, color it **red**. If it has the long **a** sound, color it **yellow**.

ă   ā

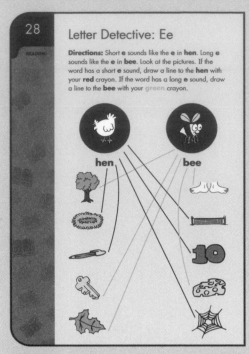

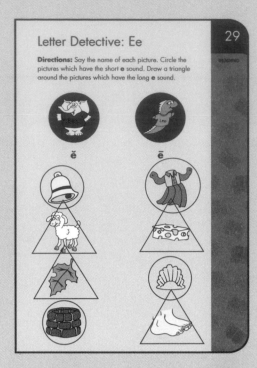

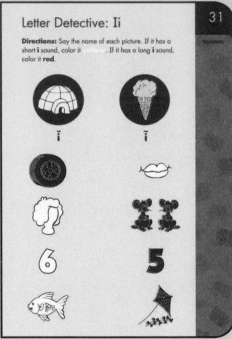

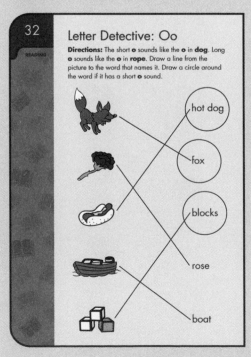

34 — Letter Detective: Uu

Directions: The short **u** sounds like the **u** in **bug**. The long **u** sounds like the **u** in **blue**. Draw a circle around the words with short **u**. Draw an **X** on the words with long **u**.

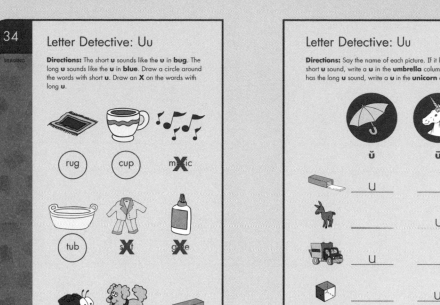

rug cup m**X**ic

tub **X**t g**X**e

bug puppy gum

35 — Letter Detective: Uu

Directions: Say the name of each picture. If it has the short **u** sound, write a **u** in the **umbrella** column. If it has the long **u** sound, write a **u** in the **unicorn** column.

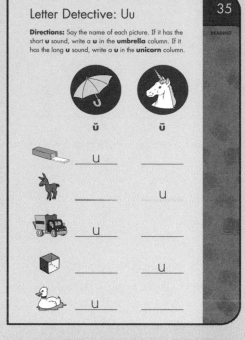

ŭ   ū

___ u ___   _____
_____   ___ u ___
___ u ___   _____
_____   ___ u ___
___ u ___   _____

36 — Super Silent E

When you add an **e** to the end of some words, the vowel changes from a short vowel sound to a long vowel sound. The **e** is silent.

Example: rip + **e** = ripe

Directions: Say the word under the first picture in each pair. Then, add an **e** to the word under the next picture. Say the new word.

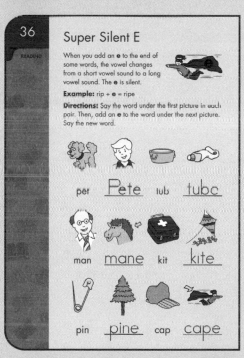

per   _Pete_   tub   _tube_

man   _mane_   kit   _kite_

pin   _pine_   cap   _cape_

37 — Sort It Out

Directions: Cut out the pictures below. If the vowel has a **long** sound, glue it on the **long** vowel side. If the vowel has a **short** sound, glue it on the **short** vowel side.

Short   **Long**

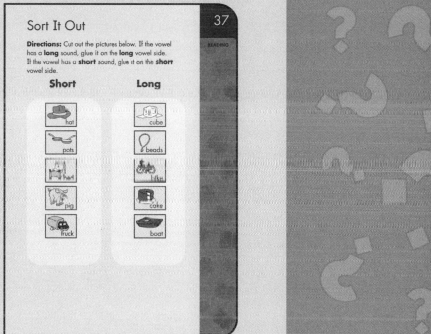

hat   cube
pots   beads
hen   bike
pig   cake
truck   boat

39 — My Vowel List

Keep this list handy and add more words to it.

short a
(ă as in cat)

long a
(ā as in train)

short e
(ĕ as in get)

long e
(ē as in tree)

short i
(ĭ as in pin)

Answers will vary

short o
(ŏ as in cot)

long o
(ō as in boat)

short u
(ŭ as in cut)

long u
(ū as in cube)

41 — Review

Directions: Color all of the vowels **black** to discover something hidden in the puzzle.

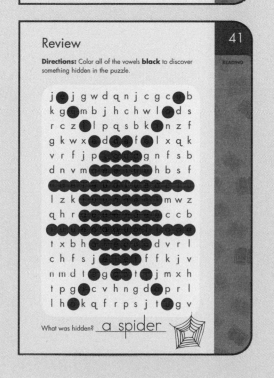

j e j g w d q n j c g c b
k g a m b j h c h w l e d s
r c z e l p q s b k n z f
g k w x a d a f e l x q k
v r f j p a a a g n f s b
d n v m a a a a a h b s f
a a a a a a a a a a a a
l z k a a a a a m w z
q h r a a a a a a c c b
a a a a a a a a a a a
t x b h a a a a d v r l
c h f s j a a f f k j v
n m d t e g a t j m x h
t p g e c v h n g d e p r l
l h e k q f r p s j t g v

What was hidden? _a spider_

42 Review

Directions: Write the vowel on each line that completes the word.

a e i o u

c <u>a</u> t

b <u>i</u> k <u>e</u>

sm <u>o</u> k <u>e</u>

tr <u>ee</u>

d <u>u</u> ck

p <u>i</u> n

m <u>o</u> m

b <u>i</u> b

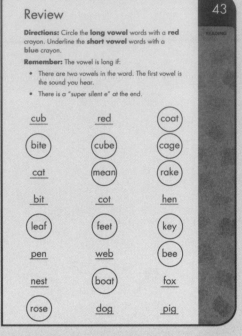

Review 43

Directions: Circle the **long vowel** words with a **red** crayon. Underline the **short vowel** words with a **blue** crayon.

Remember: The vowel is long if:
- There are two vowels in the word. The first vowel is the sound you hear.
- There is a "super silent e" at the end.

<u>cub</u> <u>red</u> (coat)

(bite) (cube) (cage)

<u>cat</u> (mean) (rake)

<u>bit</u> <u>cot</u> <u>hen</u>

(leaf) (feet) <u>key</u>

<u>pen</u> <u>web</u> (bee)

<u>nest</u> (boat) <u>fox</u>

(rose) <u>dog</u> <u>pig</u>

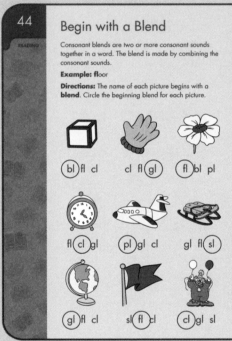

44 Begin with a Blend

Consonant blends are two or more consonant sounds together in a word. The blend is made by combining the consonant sounds.

Example: floor

Directions: The name of each picture begins with a **blend**. Circle the beginning blend for each picture.

bl (fl) cl   cl fl (gl)   (fl) bl pl

fl (cl) gl   (pl) gl cl   gl fl (sl)

(gl) fl cl   sl (fl) cl   (cl) gl sl

Blend in the Blank 45

Directions: The beginning blend for each word is missing. Fill in the correct blend to finish the word. Draw a line from the word to the picture.

<u>tr</u> ain

<u>fr</u> og

<u>dr</u> um

<u>br</u> ush

<u>pr</u> esent

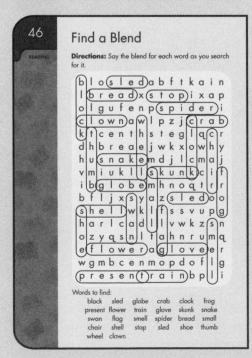

46 Find a Blend

Directions: Say the blend for each word as you search for it.

```
b l o s l e d a b f t k a i n
l b r e a d x s t o p i x a p
o l g u f e n p s p i d e r i
c l o w n a w l p z j c r a b
k t c e n t h s t e g l q c r
d h b r e a e j w k x o w h y
h u s n a k e m d j l c m a j
v m i u k l l s k u n k c i f
i b g l o b e m h n o q t r r
b f l j x s y a z s l e d o o
s h e l l w k l f s s v u p g
h a r l c a d l l v w k z s n
o z y q s n l i a h n r u m q
e f l o w e r a g l o v e r
w g m b c e n m o p d o f l g
p r e s e n t r a i n b p l i
```

Words to find:

block   sled   globe   crab   clock   frog
present flower train   glove   skunk   snake
swan   flag   smell   spider bread   small
chair   shell   stop   sled   shoe   thumb
wheel   clown

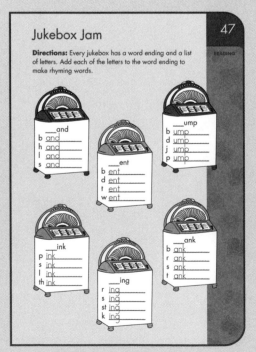

Jukebox Jam 47

Directions: Every jukebox has a word ending and a list of letters. Add each of the letters to the word ending to make rhyming words.

___and
b <u>and</u>
h <u>and</u>
l <u>and</u>
s <u>and</u>

___ump
b <u>ump</u>
d <u>ump</u>
j <u>ump</u>
p <u>ump</u>

___ent
b <u>ent</u>
d <u>ent</u>
t <u>ent</u>
w <u>ent</u>

___ink
p <u>ink</u>
s <u>ink</u>
l <u>ink</u>
th <u>ink</u>

___ing
r <u>ing</u>
s <u>ing</u>
st <u>ing</u>
k <u>ing</u>

___ank
b <u>ank</u>
r <u>ank</u>
s <u>ank</u>
t <u>ank</u>

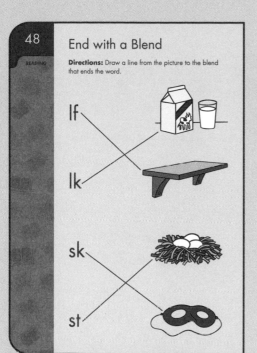

48

End with a Blend

Directions: Draw a line from the picture to the blend that ends the word.

lf

lk

sk

st

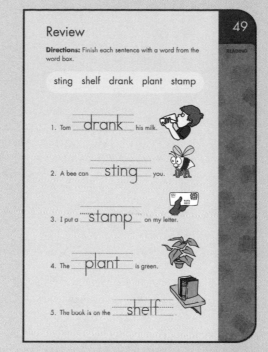

49

Review

Directions: Finish each sentence with a word from the word box.

sting shelf drank plant stamp

1. Tom _drank_ his milk.

2. A bee can _sting_ you.

3. I put a _stamp_ on my letter.

4. The _plant_ is green.

5. The book is on the _shelf_.

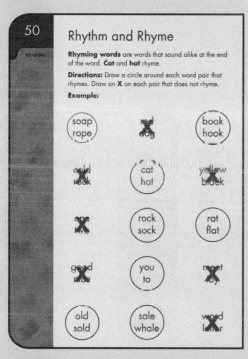

50

Rhythm and Rhyme

Rhyming words are words that sound alike at the end of the word. **Cat** and **hat** rhyme.

Directions: Draw a circle around each word pair that rhymes. Draw an **X** on each pair that does not rhyme.

Example:

(soap rope)   ~~red dog~~ X   (book hook)

~~cold rock~~ X   (cat hat)   ~~yellow black~~ X

~~hive~~ X   (rock sock)   (rat flat)

~~good prize~~ X   (you to)   ~~most toy~~ X

(old sold)   (sale whale)   ~~word letter~~ X

51

Rhythm and Rhyme

Rhyming words are words that sound alike at the end of the word

Directions: Draw a line to match the pictures that rhyme. Write two of your rhyming word pairs below.

Answers will vary

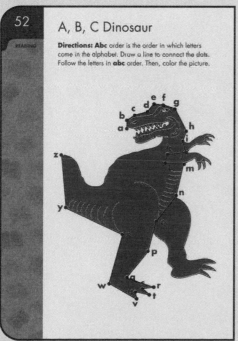

52

A, B, C Dinosaur

Directions: **Abc** order is the order in which letters come in the alphabet. Draw a line to connect the dots. Follow the letters in **abc** order. Then, color the picture.

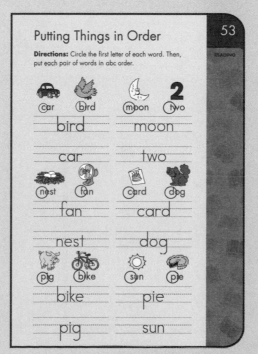

53

Putting Things in Order

Directions: Circle the first letter of each word. Then, put each pair of words in abc order.

(c)ar   (b)ird   (m)oon   (t)wo

bird   _moon_

car   _two_

(n)est   (f)an   (c)ard   (d)og

fan   _card_

nest   _dog_

(p)ig   (b)ike   (s)un   (p)ie

bike   _pie_

pig   _sun_

54 Two Words in One

Compound words are two words that are put together to make one new word.

Directions: Look at the pictures and the two words that are next to each other. Put the words together to make a new word. Write the new word.

Example:

house + boat = **houseboat**

side + walk = **sidewalk**

lip + stick = **lipstick**

sand + box = **sandbox**

lunch + box = **lunchbox**

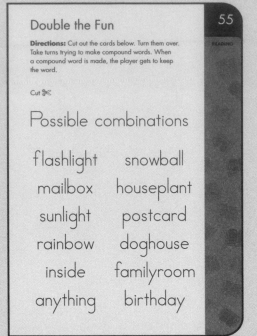

Double the Fun 55

Directions: Cut out the cards below. Turn them over. Take turns trying to make compound words. When a compound word is made, the player gets to keep the word.

Cut ✄

Possible combinations

flashlight   snowball

mailbox   houseplant

sunlight   postcard

rainbow   doghouse

inside   familyroom

anything   birthday

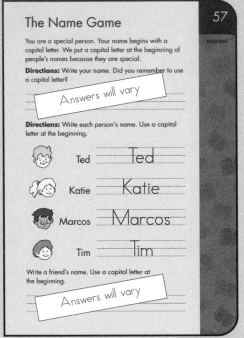

The Name Game 57

You are a special person. Your name begins with a capital letter. We put a capital letter at the beginning of people's names because they are special.

Directions: Write your name. Did you remember to use a capital letter?

Answers will vary

Directions: Write each person's name. Use a capital letter at the beginning.

Ted — **Ted**

Katie — **Katie**

Marcos — **Marcos**

Tim — **Tim**

Write a friend's name. Use a capital letter at the beginning.

Answers will vary

58 7 Delightful Days

The days of the week begin with capital letters.

Directions: Write the days of the week in the spaces below. Put them in order. Be sure to start with capital letters.

Tuesday	Sunday
Saturday	Monday
Monday	Tuesday
Friday	Wednesday
Thursday	Thursday
Sunday	Friday
Wednesday	Saturday

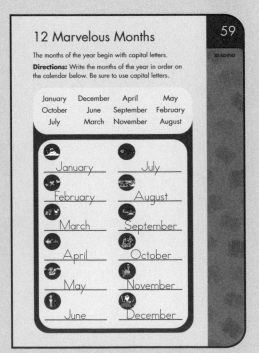

12 Marvelous Months 59

The months of the year begin with capital letters.

Directions: Write the months of the year in order on the calendar below. Be sure to use capital letters.

January	December	April	May
October	June	September	February
July	March	November	August

January   July

February   August

March   September

April   October

May   November

June   December

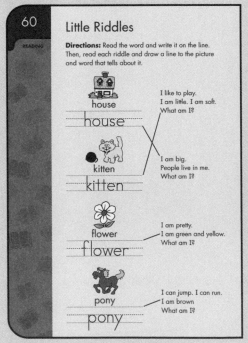

60 Little Riddles

Directions: Read the word and write it on the line. Then, read each riddle and draw a line to the picture and word that tells about it.

house

house

I like to play.
I am little. I am soft.
What am I?

kitten

kitten

I am big.
People live in me.
What am I?

flower

flower

I am pretty.
I am green and yellow.
What am I?

pony

pony

I can jump. I can run.
I am brown
What am I?

61 Get the Picture?

Directions: Read the sentence. Circle the word that makes sense. Use the picture clues to help you. Then, write the word.

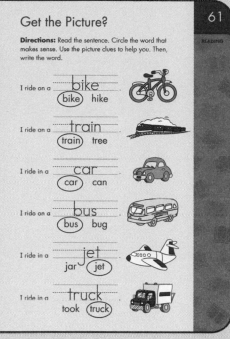

I ride on a **bike** (bike) hike

I ride on a **train** (train) tree

I ride in a **car** (car) can

I ride on a **bus** (bus) bug

I ride in a **jet** jar (jet)

I ride in a **truck** took (truck)

62 Winter Warmers

Directions: Color the things that keep you warm.

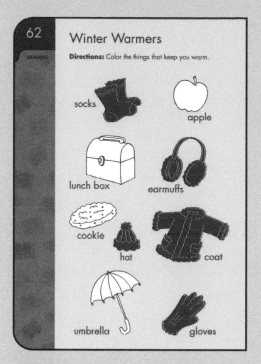

socks apple lunch box earmuffs cookie hat coat umbrella gloves

63 Sunlight, Moonlight

Directions: Write the words from the box under the pictures they describe.

stars sun moon rays
dark light night day

stars — sun
moon — rays
dark — light
night — day

64 Like It or Not

Directions: Circle the picture in each row that is most like the first picture.
Example:

carrot jacks bread pea

baseball sneakers basketball bat

store school home bakery

kitten dog fox cat

65 Odd One Out

Directions: Draw an **X** on the picture that does not belong in each group.

fruit
apple peach corn (X) watermelon

wild animals
bear kitten (X) gorilla lion

pets
cat fish elephant (X) dog

flowers
grass (X) rose daisy tulip

66 See It, Sort It

Directions: Write each word in the correct row at the bottom of the page.

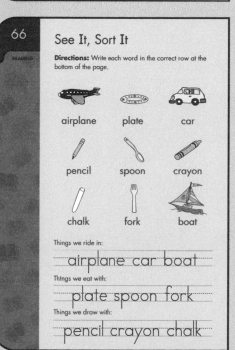

airplane plate car
pencil spoon crayon
chalk fork boat

Things we ride in:
airplane car boat

Things we eat with:
plate spoon fork

Things we draw with:
pencil crayon chalk

Time to Rhyme

Directions: Circle the pictures in each row that rhyme.

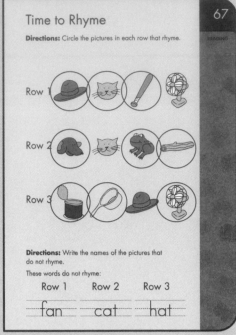

Row 1

Row 2

Row 3

Directions: Write the names of the pictures that do not rhyme.

These words do not rhyme:

Row 1   Row 2   Row 3

fan   cat   hat

Twice the Fun!

Directions: Read the story. Then, use the words in the box and the picture to write your answers.

Ben and Ann are twin babies. They were born at the same time. They have the same mother. Ben is a boy baby. Ann is a girl baby.

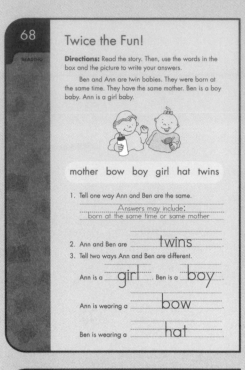

mother   bow   boy   girl   hat   twins

1. Tell one way Ann and Ben are the same.

   Answers may include: born at the same time or same mother

2. Ann and Ben are   **twins**
3. Tell two ways Ann and Ben are different.

   Ann is a   **girl**   Ben is a   **boy**

   Ann is wearing a   **bow**

   Ben is wearing a   **hat**

Map It!

Directions: Color the path the girl should take to go home. Use the sentences to help you.

1. Go to the school and turn left.
2. At the end of the street, turn right.
3. Walk past the park and turn right.
4. After you pass the pool, turn right.

Make a Snowman!

Directions: Write the number of the sentence that goes with each picture in the circle.

1. Roll a large snowball for the snowman's bottom.
2. Make another snowball and put it on top of the first.
3. Put the last snowball on top.
4. Dress the snowman.

How Does Your Garden Grow?

Directions: Read the story. Then, write the steps to grow a flower.

First find a sunny spot. Then, plant the seed. Water it. The flower will start to grow. Pull the weeds around it. Remember to keep giving the flower water. Enjoy your flower.

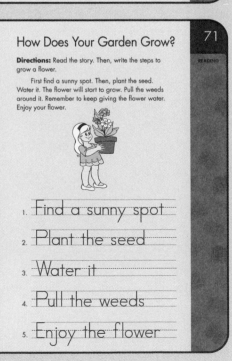

1. Find a sunny spot
2. Plant the seed
3. Water it
4. Pull the weeds
5. Enjoy the flower

On the Pond

Directions: Look at the picture. Write the words from the box to finish the sentences.

frog   log   bird   fish   ducks

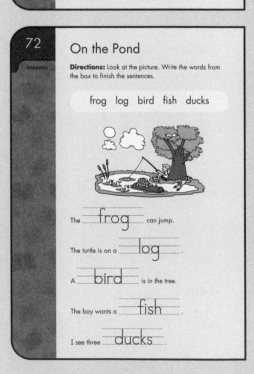

The   **frog**   can jump.

The turtle is on a   **log** .

A   **bird**   is in the tree.

The boy wants a   **fish** .

I see three   **ducks** .

73 — An Apple a Day

Directions: Read about apples. Then, write the answers.

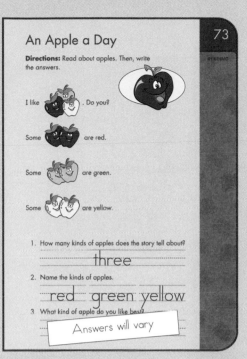

I like ___. Do you?

Some ___ are red.

Some ___ are green.

Some ___ are yellow.

1. How many kinds of apples does the story tell about?
   three
2. Name the kinds of apples.
   red green yellow
3. What kind of apple do you like best?
   Answers will vary

74 — Puddle Jumping

Directions: Read the story. Write the words from the story that complete each sentence.

Jada and Bill like to play in the rain. They take off their shoes and socks. They splash in the puddles. It feels cold! It is fun to splash!

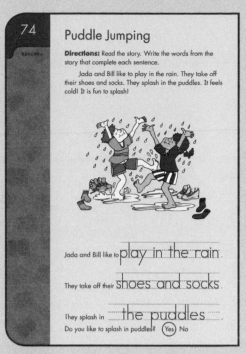

Jada and Bill like to **play in the rain**.

They take off their **shoes and socks**.

They splash in **the puddles**.

Do you like to splash in puddles? **(Yes)** No

75 — Falling Leaves

Directions: Read about raking leaves. Then, answer the questions.

I like to rake leaves. Do you? Leaves die each year. They get brown and dry. They fall from the trees. Then, we rake them up.

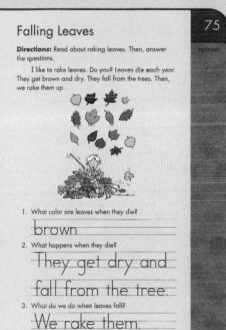

1. What color are leaves when they die?
   brown
2. What happens when they die?
   They get dry and fall from the tree.
3. What do we do when leaves fall?
   We rake them.

76 — Bunches of Balloons

Directions: Read the story. Then, answer the questions.

Some balloons float. They are filled with gas. Some do not float. They are filled with air. Some clowns carry balloons. Balloons come in many colors. What color do you like?

1. What makes balloons float? **gas**
2. What is in balloons that do not float? **air**
3. What shape are the balloons the clown is holding? **circle**

77 — Time to Party!

Directions: Read about the party. Then, complete the invitation.

The party will be at Dog's house. The party will start at 1:00 P.M. It will last 2 hours. Write your birthday for the date of the party.

Party Invitation

Where: **Dog's house**

Answers will vary

Time It Begins: **1:00** P.M.

Time It Ends: **3:00** P.M.

Answers will vary

Directions: On the last line, write something else about the party.

78 — Review

Directions: Read the story. Then, circle the pictures of things that are wet.

Some things used in baking are dry. Some things used in baking are wet. To bake a cake, first mix the salt, sugar and flour. Then, add the egg. Now, add the milk. Stir. Put the cake in the oven.

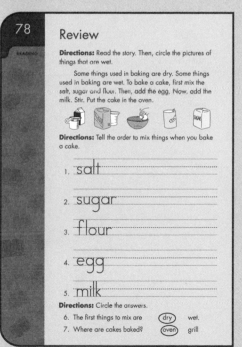

Directions: Tell the order to mix things when you bake a cake.

1. **salt**
2. **sugar**
3. **flour**
4. **egg**
5. **milk**

Directions: Circle the answers.

6. The first things to mix are **(dry)** wet.
7. Where are cakes baked? **(oven)** grill

A Tiger Tale

79
READING

Directions: Read about tigers. Then, write the answers.

Tigers sleep during the day. They hunt at night. Tigers eat meat. They hunt deer. They like to eat wild pigs. If they cannot find meat, tigers will eat fish.

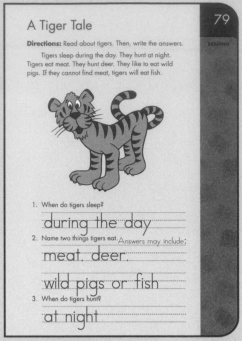

1. When do tigers sleep?

during the day

2. Name two things tigers eat. Answers may include:

meat, deer,

wild pigs or fish

3. When do tigers hunt?

at night

Get a Clue

80
READING

Directions: Read the story about tigers again. Then, complete the puzzle.

¹F I ²S H
　　L
³M E A T
　　E
⁴P I G

Across

1. When tigers cannot get meat, they eat _____.
3. The food tigers like best is _____.
4. Tigers like to eat this meat: wild _____.

Down

2. Tigers do this during the day.

Tiger Art

81
READING

Directions: Follow directions to complete the picture of the tiger.

1. Draw **black** stripes on the tiger's body and tail.
2. Color the tiger's tongue **red**.
3. Draw claws on the feet.
4. Draw a **black** nose and two **black** eyes on the tiger's face.
5. Color the rest of the tiger orange.
6. Draw tall, green grass for the tiger to sleep in.

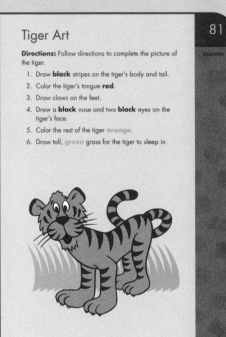

Simon Says

82
READING

Directions: Read how to play Simon Says. Then, answer the questions.

Simon Says

Here is how to play Simon Says: One kid is Simon. Simon is the leader. Everyone must do what Simon says and does buy only if the leader says, "Simon says" first. Let's try it. "Simon says, 'Pat your head.'" "Simon says, 'Pat your nose. Pat your toes.'" Oops! Did you pat your toes? I did not say, "Simon says," first. If you patted your toes, you are out!

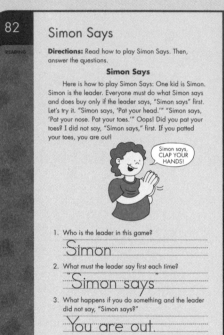

Simon says, CLAP YOUR HANDS!

1. Who is the leader in this game?

Simon

2. What must the leader say first each time?

"Simon says"

3. What happens if you do something and the leader did not say, "Simon says?"

You are out.

Eyes on Simon

83
READING

Directions: Read each sentence. Look at the picture next to it. Circle the picture if the person is playing Simon Says correctly.

1. Simon says, "Put your hands on your hips."

2. Simon says, "Stand on one leg."

3. Simon says, "Put your hands on your head."

4. Simon says, "Ride a bike."

5. Simon says, "Jump up and down."

6. Simon says, "Pet a dog."

A Message from Simon

84
READING

Directions: Read the sentences. If Simon tells you to do something, follow the directions. If Simon does not tell you to do something, go to the next sentence.

1. Simon says: Cross out all the numbers 2 through 9.
2. Simon says: Cross out the vowel that is in the word "sun".
3. Cross out the letter "B".
4. Cross out the vowels "A" and "E."
5. Simon says: Cross out the consonants in the word "cup."
6. Cross out the letter "Z."
7. Simon says: Cross out all the "K's."

Answer: Great job

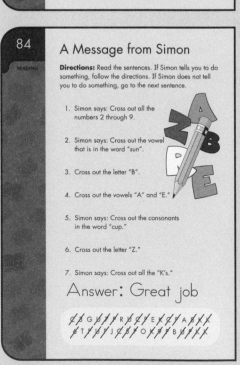

Boats Afloat

Directions: Read about boats. Then, answer the questions.

See the boats! They float on water. Some boats have sails. The wind moves the sails. It makes the boats go. Many people name their sailboats. They paint the name on the side of the boat.

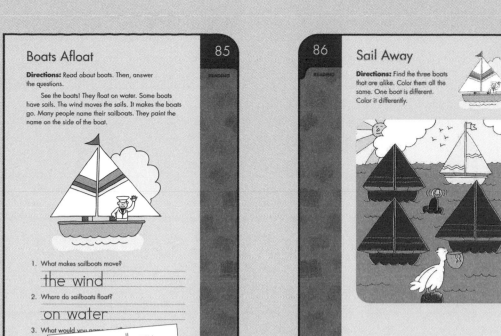

1. What makes sailboats move?

the wind

2. Where do sailboats float?

on water

3. What would you name

Answers will vary

Sail Away

Directions: Find the three boats that are alike. Color them all the same. One boat is different. Color it differently.

Gone to Sea

Directions: Write a sentence under each picture to tell what is happening. Read the story you wrote.

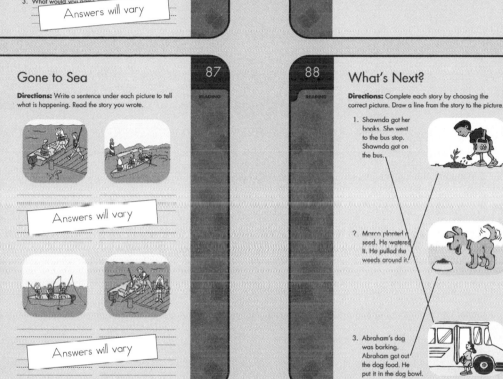

Answers will vary

Answers will vary

What's Next?

Directions: Complete each story by choosing the correct picture. Draw a line from the story to the picture.

1. Shawnda got her books. She went to the bus stop. Shawnda got on the bus.

2. Marco planted a seed. He watered it. He pulled the weeds around it.

3. Abraham's dog was barking. Abraham got out the dog food. He put it in the dog bowl.

A Happy Ending

Directions: Read each story. Circle the sentence that tells how the story will end.

Ann was riding her bike. She saw a dog in the park. She stopped to pet it. Ann left to go home.

The dog went swimming.

(The dog followed Ann.)

The dog went home with a cat.

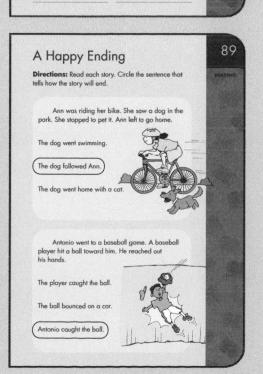

Antonio went to a baseball game. A baseball player hit a ball toward him. He reached out his hands.

The player caught the ball.

The ball bounced on a car.

(Antonio caught the ball.)

How Would You Feel?

Directions: Read each story. Choose a word from the box to show how each person feels.

happy   excited   sad   mad

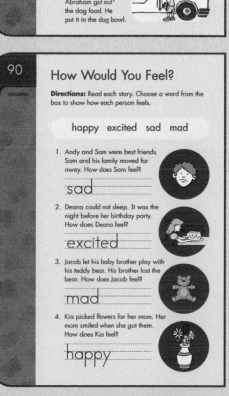

1. Andy and Sam were best friends. Sam and his family moved far away. How does Sam feel?

sad

2. Deana could not sleep. It was the night before her birthday party. How does Deana feel?

excited

3. Jacob let his baby brother play with his teddy bear. His brother lost the bear. How does Jacob feel?

mad

4. Kia picked flowers for her mom. Her mom smiled when she got them. How does Kia feel?

happy

92 Nouns All Around

ENGLISH

Directions: Write these naming words in the correct box.

store zoo child baby
teacher table cat park
gym woman sock horse

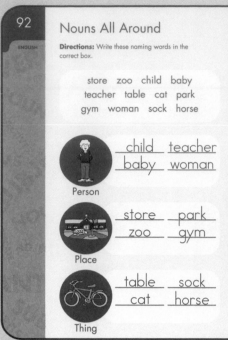

Person: child   teacher   baby   woman

Place: store   park   zoo   gym

Thing: table   sock   cat   horse

93 Pick a Pair

ENGLISH

Some nouns name things that go together.

Directions: Draw a line to match the nouns on the left with the things they go with on the right.

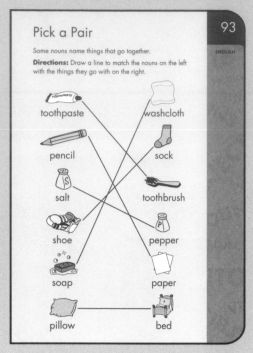

toothpaste — washcloth
pencil — sock
salt — toothbrush
shoe — pepper
soap — paper
pillow — bed

94 Get in on the Action

ENGLISH

Directions: Look at the picture and read the words. Write an action word in each sentence below.

swing   rings
kick
run   talk

1. The two boys like to ___talk___ together.

2. The children ___kick___ the soccer ball.

3. Some children like to ___swing___ on the swing.

4. The girl can ___run___ very fast.

5. The teacher ___rings___ the bell.

95 Review

ENGLISH

Directions: Read the sentences below. Draw a **red** circle around the nouns. Draw a **blue** line under the verbs.

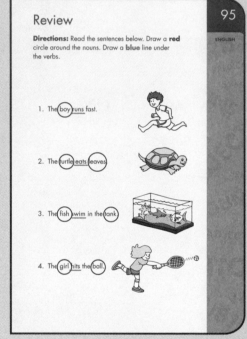

1. The boy runs fast.

2. The turtle eats leaves.

3. The fish swim in the tank.

4. The girl hits the ball.

96 Show and Tell

ENGLISH

Directions: Read the words in the box. Choose the word that describes the picture. Write it next to the picture.

wet round funny soft sad tall

soft
tall
funny
sad
round
wet

97 Picture Perfect

ENGLISH

Colors and numbers can describe nouns.

Directions: Underline the describing word in each sentence. Draw a picture to go with each sentence.

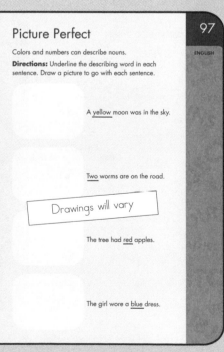

A yellow moon was in the sky.

Two worms are on the road.

Drawings will vary

The tree had red apples.

The girl wore a blue dress.

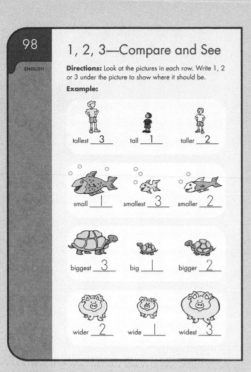

98
ENGLISH

1, 2, 3—Compare and See

Directions: Look at the pictures in each row. Write 1, 2 or 3 under the picture to show where it should be.

Example:

tallest **3**   tall **1**   taller **2**

small **1**   smallest **3**   smaller **2**

biggest **3**   big **1**   bigger **2**

wider **2**   wide **1**   widest **3**

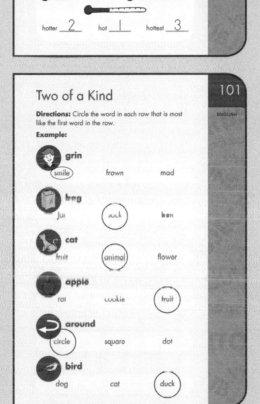

1, 2, 3—Compare and See

99
ENGLISH

Directions: Look at the pictures in each row. Write 1, 2 or 3 under the picture to show where it should be.

shortest **3**   shorter **2**   short **1**

longest **3**   longer **2**   long **1**

happy **1**   happier **2**   happiest **3**

hotter **2**   hot **1**   hottest **3**

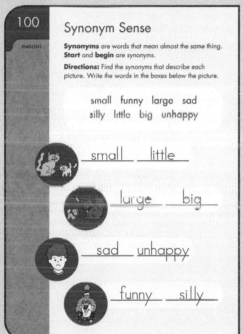

100
ENGLISH

Synonym Sense

Synonyms are words that mean almost the same thing. **Start** and **begin** are synonyms.

Directions: Find the synonyms that describe each picture. Write the words in the boxes below the picture.

small   funny   large   sad
silly   little   big   unhappy

small   little

large   big

sad   unhappy

funny   silly

Two of a Kind

101
ENGLISH

Directions: Circle the word in each row that is most like the first word in the row.

Example:

grin
(smile)   frown   mad

beg
jut   (ask)   loan

cat
fruit   (animal)   flower

apple
rat   cookie   (fruit)

around
(circle)   square   dot

bird
dog   cat   (duck)

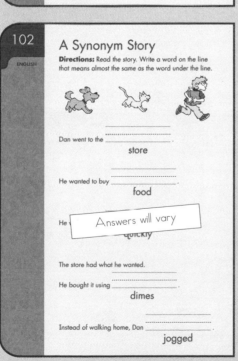

102
ENGLISH

A Synonym Story

Directions: Read the story. Write a word on the line that means almost the same as the word under the line.

Dan went to the _____ .
store

He wanted to buy _____ .
food

He _____ | Answers will vary |
quickly

The store had what he wanted. _____

He bought it using _____ .
dimes

Instead of walking home, Dan _____
jogged

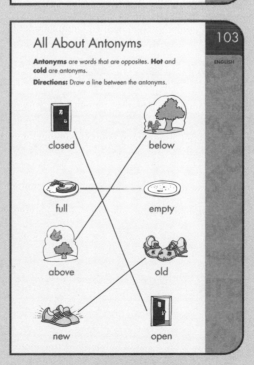

All About Antonyms

103
ENGLISH

Antonyms are words that are opposites. **Hot** and **cold** are antonyms.

Directions: Draw a line between the antonyms.

closed   below

full   empty

above   old

new   open

104 Opposites Attract

Directions: Circle the picture in each row that is the opposite of the first picture.

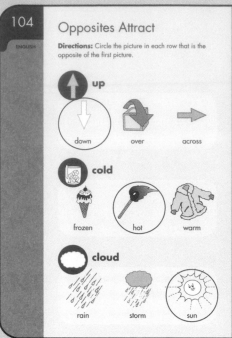

up

down   over   across

cold

frozen   hot   warm

cloud

rain   storm   sun

105 Fishing for Antonyms

Directions: Read each clue. Write the answers in the puzzle.

high   yes   left
heavy   tight
safe   full

Across:
1. Opposite of low
2. Opposite of no
4. Opposite of empty
6. Opposite of loose

Down:
1. Opposite of light
3. Opposite of dangerous
5. Opposite of right

106 Sound Alikes

Homophones are words that **sound** the same but are spelled differently and mean something different. **Blew** and **blue** are homophones.

Directions: Look at the word pairs. Choose the word that describes the picture. Write the word on the line next to the picture.

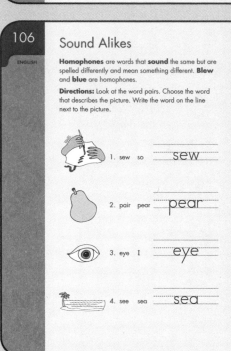

1. sew so   sew

2. pair pear   pear

3. eye I   eye

4. see sea   sea

107 Sound Alikes

Directions: Read each sentence. Underline the two words that sound the same but are spelled differently and mean something different.

1. Tom <u>ate</u> <u>eight</u> grapes.

2. Becky <u>read</u> *Little <u>Red</u> Riding Hood.*

3. I went <u>to</u> buy <u>two</u> dolls.

4. Five <u>blue</u> feathers <u>blew</u> in the wind.

5. <u>Would</u> you get <u>wood</u> for the fire?

108 Say it with a Sentence

Sentences begin with capital letters.

Directions: Read the sentences and write them below. Begin each sentence with a capital letter.

Example:

the cat is fat.

The cat is fat.

my dog is big.

My dog is big.

the boy is sad.

The boy is sad.

bikes are fun!

Bikes are fun!

dad can bake.

Dad can bake.

109 All in Order

If you change the order of the words in a sentence, you can change the meaning of a sentence.

Directions: Read the sentences. Draw a circle around the sentence that describes the picture.

Example:

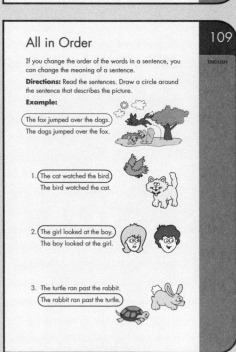

(The fox jumped over the dogs.)
The dogs jumped over the fox.

1. (The cat watched the bird.)
   The bird watched the cat.

2. (The girl looked at the boy.)
   The boy looked at the girl.

3. The turtle ran past the rabbit.
   (The rabbit ran past the turtle.)

110 — Lemonade for Sale!

Directions: Look at the picture. Put the words in order. Write the sentences on the lines below.

1. We made lemonade. some
2. good. It was
3. We the sold lemonade.
4. cost It five cents.
5. fun. We had

1. We made some lemonade.
2. It was good.
3. We sold the lemonade.
4. It cost five cents.
5. We had fun.

111 — Telling Sentences: Pet Crazy

Directions: Read the sentences and write them below. Begin each sentence with a capital letter. End each sentence with a period.

1. most children like pets
2. some children like dogs
3. some children like cats
4. some children like snakes
5. some children like all animals

1. Most children like pets.
2. Some children like dogs.
3. Some children like cats.
4. Some children like snakes.
5. Some children like all animals.

112 — Telling Sentences: Going Shopping

Directions: Read the sentences and write them below. Begin each sentence with a capital letter. End each sentence with a period.

1. i like to go to the store with Mom
2. we go on Friday
3. i get to push the cart
4. i get to buy the cookies
5. I like to help Mom

1. I like to go to the store with Mom.
2. We go on Friday.
3. I get to push the cart.
4. I get to buy the cookies.
5. I like to help Mom.

113 — Asking Sentences: Monkeying Around

Directions: Write the first word of each asking sentence. Be sure to begin each question with a capital letter. End each question with a question mark.

1. Do you like the zoo? — do
2. How much does it cost? — how
3. Can you feed the ducks? — can
4. Will you see the monkeys? — will
5. What time will you eat lunch? — what

114 — Asking Sentences: Getting to Know You

Directions: Read the asking sentences. Write the sentences below. Begin each sentence with a capital letter. End each sentence with a question mark.

1. what game will we play
2. do you like to read
3. how old are you
4. who is your best friend
5. can you tie your shoes

1. What game will we play?
2. Do you like to read?
3. How old are you?
4. Who is your best friend?
5. Can you tie your shoes?

115 — Punctuation Parade

Directions: Put a period or a question mark at the end of each sentence below.

1. Do you like parades?
2. The clowns lead the parade.
3. Can you hear the band?
4. The balloons are big.
5. Can you see the horses?

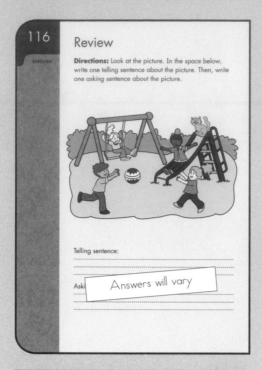

116 ENGLISH **Review**

Directions: Look at the picture. In the space below, write one telling sentence about the picture. Then, write one asking sentence about the picture.

Telling sentence:

Ask Answers will vary

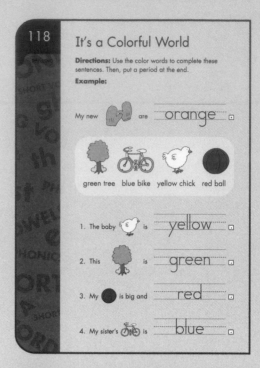

118 **It's a Colorful World**

Directions: Use the color words to complete these sentences. Then, put a period at the end.

Example:

My new [mittens] are orange .

green tree   blue bike   yellow chick   red ball

1. The baby [chick] is yellow .
2. This [tree] is green .
3. My [ball] is big and red .
4. My sister's [bike] is blue .

Finish the Pictures **119**

Directions: Read the words. Finish the pictures.

a red ball   a black hat

a yellow sun   a pink kite

an orange balloon   a blue umbrella

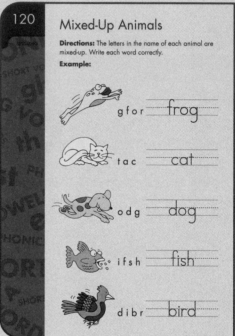

120 **Mixed-Up Animals**

Directions: The letters in the name of each animal are mixed-up. Write each word correctly.

Example:

g f o r   frog

t a c   cat

o d g   dog

i f s h   fish

d i b r   bird

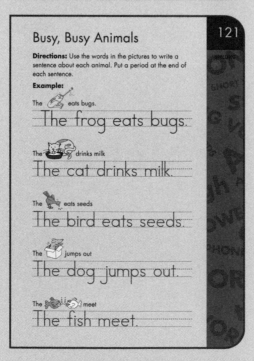

Busy, Busy Animals **121**

Directions: Use the words in the pictures to write a sentence about each animal. Put a period at the end of each sentence.

Example:

The [frog] eats bugs.
The frog eats bugs.

The [cat] drinks milk
The cat drinks milk.

The [bird] eats seeds
The bird eats seeds.

The [dog] jumps out
The dog jumps out.

The [fish] meet
The fish meet.

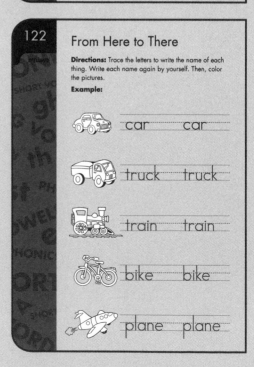

122 **From Here to There**

Directions: Trace the letters to write the name of each thing. Write each name again by yourself. Then, color the pictures.

Example:

car   car

truck   truck

train   train

bike   bike

plane   plane

On the Go · 123

Directions: Say the name of each thing. Write the beginning sound under its name. Find two pictures in each row that begin with the same sound as the first picture. Write the same first letter under them.

Example:

car
c
c   c

train
t
t

bike
b
b   b

plane
p
p   p

124 · Time to Get Dressed

Directions: Trace the letters to write the name of each clothing word. Then, write each name again by yourself.

Example:

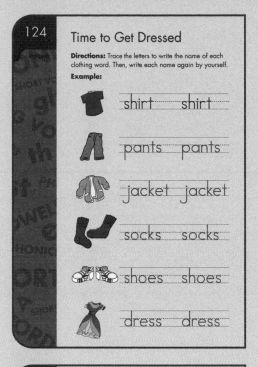

shirt   shirt

pants   pants

jacket   jacket

socks   socks

shoes   shoes

dress   dress

Matching Clothes · 125

Directions: Some of these sentences tell a whole idea. Others have something missing. If something is missing, draw a line to the word that completes the sentence. Put a period at the end of each sentence.

Example:

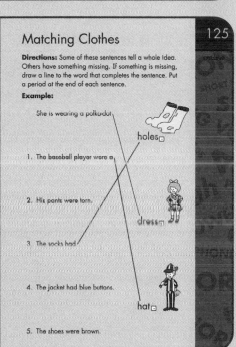

She is wearing a polka-dot

holes.

1. The baseball player wore a

2. His pants were torn.

dress.

3. The socks had

4. The jacket had blue buttons.

hat.

5. The shoes were brown.

126 · A Bite to Eat

Directions: Trace the letters to write the name of each food word. Write each name again by yourself. Then, color the pictures.

Example:

bread   bread

cookie   cookie

apple   apple

cake   cake

milk   milk

egg   egg

What's for Lunch? · 127

Directions: Write the food names in the story.

Kim got up in the morning.

"Do you want an ___egg___ ?"
her mother asked.

"Yes, please," Kim said.

"May I have some ___milk___ , too?"

"Okay," her mother said.

"How about some ___ice cream___ ?"
Kim asked with a smile.

Her mother laughed. "Not now," she said.

She put an ___apple___ in Kim's lunch.

"Do you want a ___cookie___ or some

___cake___ today?"

"Both!" Kim said.

128 · 1, 2, 3 Spell!

Directions: Trace the letters to write the name of each number. Write the numbers again by yourself. Then, color the number pictures.

Example:

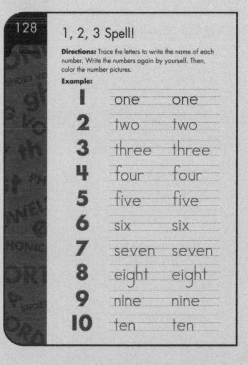

1   one   one
2   two   two
3   three   three
4   four   four
5   five   five
6   six   six
7   seven   seven
8   eight   eight
9   nine   nine
10   ten   ten

129 How Many?

Directions: Use the number words to answer each question.

1. How many eyes do you have?
two

2. How many mouths do you have?
one

3. How many fingers do you have?
ten

4. How many wheels are on a car?
four

5. How many peas are in the pod?
three

6. How many cups do you see?
six

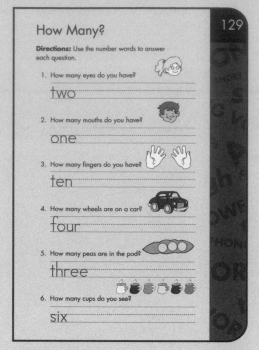

130 Spelling in Action

Directions: Circle the word that is spelled correctly. Then, write the correct spelling in the blank.

Example:

seep / (sleep) / slep — **sleep**

paly / pay / (play) — **play**

seee / cee / (see) — **see**

rum / (run) / runn — **run**

(jump) / jumb / junp — **jump**

131 Spelling in Action

To show more than one of something, add **s** to the end of the word.

Example: one cat   two cats

Directions: In each sentence, add **s** to show more than one. Then, write the action word that completes each sentence.

sit jump stop ride

Example:
The frog **s** **sleep** in the sun.

1. The boy **s** **sit** on the fence.
2. The car **s** **stop** at the sign.
3. The girl **s** **jump** in the water.
4. The dog **s** **ride** in the wagon.

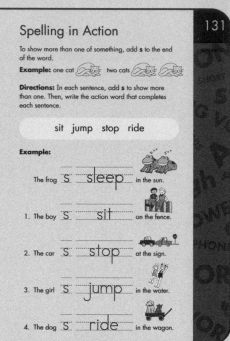

132 Makes Sense to Me!

Directions: Circle the word that is spelled correctly. Then, write the correct spelling in the blank.

Example:

tast / (taste) / tste — **taste**

(touch) / tuch / touh — **touch**

smel / smll / (smell) — **smell**

her / (hear) / har — **hear**

(see) / se / sea — **see**

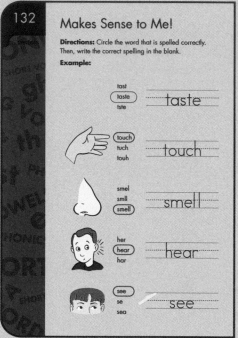

133 Makes Sense to Me!

Directions: Use the sense words in the box to answer each question.

smell see taste hear touch

1. Which word begins with the same sound as
smell

2. Which word begins with the same sound as
see

3. Which words begin with the same sound as
touch **taste**

4. Which word begins with the same sound as
hear

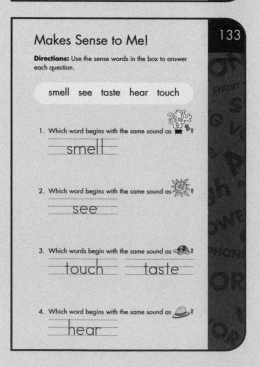

134 How's the Weather?

Directions: Write the weather word that completes each sentence. Put a period at the end of the telling sentences and a question mark at the end of the asking sentences.

Example:
Do flowers grow in the **sun** **?**

rain water wet hot

1. The sun makes me **hot** **.**
2. When it rains, the grass gets **wet** **.**
3. Do you think it will **rain** on our picnic **?**
4. Should you drink the **water** from the rain **?**

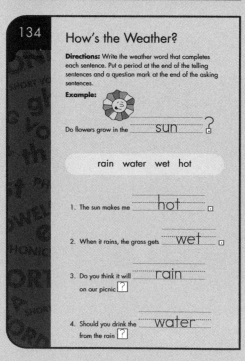

How's the Weather? 135

Directions: Write the missing words to complete the story. The first letter of each word is written for you.

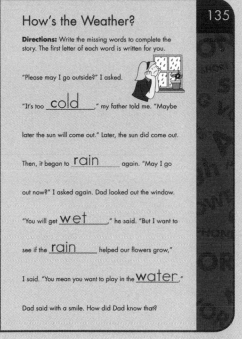

"Please may I go outside?" I asked.

"It's too __cold__," my father told me. "Maybe later the sun will come out." Later, the sun did come out.

Then, it began to __rain__ again. "May I go out now?" I asked again. Dad looked out the window.

"You will get __wet__," he said. "But I want to see if the __rain__ helped our flowers grow," I said. "You mean you want to play in the __water__," Dad said with a smile. How did Dad know that?

Head to Toe 136

Directions: Write the word that completes each sentence. Put a period at the end of the telling sentences and a question mark at the end of the asking sentences.

Example:

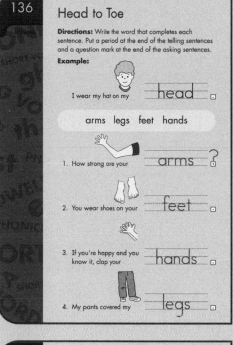

I wear my hat on my __head__.

arms   legs   feet   hands

1. How strong are your __arms__?

2. You wear shoes on your __feet__.

3. If you're happy and you know it, clap your __hands__.

4. My pants covered my __legs__.

Head to Toe 137

Directions: Read the sentence parts below. Draw a line from the first part of the sentence to the second part that completes it.

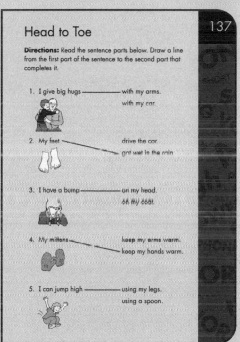

1. I give big hugs —— with my arms.
   with my car.

2. My feet —— drive the car.
   got wet in the rain.

3. I have a bump —— on my head.
   on my coat.

4. My mittens —— keep my arms warm.
   keep my hands warm.

5. I can jump high —— using my legs.
   using a spoon.

What's the Difference? 138

Some words are opposites. **Opposites** are things that are different in every way. **Dark** and **light** are opposites.

Directions: Trace the letters to write each word. Then, write the word again by yourself.

Example:

new   new
old   old

big   big
little   little

lost   lost
found   found

What's the Difference? 139

Directions: Read the sentence about the first picture. Write another sentence about the picture beside it. Use the opposite words.

Example:

This apple is little.

This apple is big.

dark   old   first   new   light   last

1. This coat is light.

This coat is dark.

2. This woman is first.

This woman is last.

3. This car is old.

This car is new.

People Power! 140

Directions: Trace the letters to write each word. Then, write the word again by yourself.

girl   girl

boy   boy

man   man

woman   woman

people   people

children   children

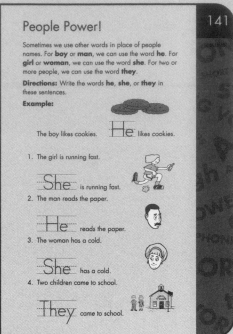

People Power!

141

Sometimes we use other words in place of people names. For **boy** or **man**, we can use the word **he**. For **girl** or **woman**, we can use the word **she**. For two or more people, we can use the word **they**.

Directions: Write the words **he, she,** or **they** in these sentences.

Example:

The boy likes cookies.   He likes cookies.

1. The girl is running fast.

   She is running fast.

2. The man reads the paper.

   He reads the paper.

3. The woman has a cold.

   She has a cold.

4. Two children came to school.

   They came to school.

142

People Power!

Directions: Write the people word that completes each sentence.

man   girl   children   boy   woman

1. The   boy   feeds the cat.

2. The   children   are buying dessert.

3. What is the   woman   painting?

4. The   man   will grow corn.

5. The dog runs to the   girl .

144

MATH

Know Your Numbers

Directions: Use the color codes to color the parrot.

Color:

1's red

2's blue

3's yellow

4's green

5's orange

Hop to It!

145

MATH

Directions: How many are there of each picture? Write the answers in the boxes. The first one is done for you.

| 7 | 4 | 10 | 5 | 3 |

146

MATH

Counting Zoo

Directions: How many are there of each shape? Write the answers in the boxes. The first one is done for you.

| 1 | 7 | 6 |
| 10 | 3 | 2 |

Number Hunt

147

MATH

Directions: Find the number words 0 through 12 hidden in the box.

```
t e a z w z x a b i g (t e n)
o l z r b e r e v e d l a j
(t w e l v e) a (b o n e) c d z
i a r p q d p s u j x e i w
c f o p l s c k i q u i i o
m s t f v i o e t f g h d
t n u w x g z w h g h r o
(n i n e) k f d (f o u r) t j f
a s g l q c w k o s n v m i
n y c e b o n h h p o m p v
b e x v (s e v e n) w e n e
(t h r e e) r t a l j k x q z
m o a (n e n i m u t w a y x
```

Words to find:

zero	four	eight	eleven
one	five	nine	twelve
two	six	ten	
three	seven		

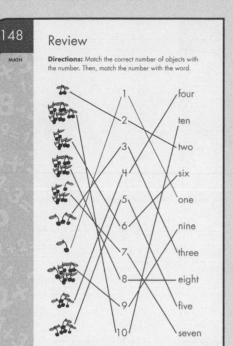

148 Review

MATH

Directions: Match the correct number of objects with the number. Then, match the number with the word.

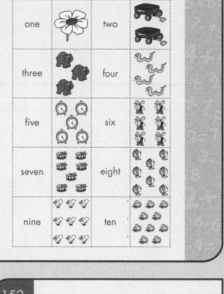

149 Mix and Match

MATH

Directions: Cut out the pictures and number words below. Mix them up and match them again.

Cut ✂

one		two	
three		four	
five		six	
seven		eight	
nine		ten	

Following Orders 151

MATH

Sequencing is putting numbers in the correct order.

1, 2, 3, 4, 5, 6, 7, 8, 9, 10

Directions: Write the missing numbers.

Example: 4, _5_, 6

3, _4_, 5   7, _8_, 9   8, _9_, 10

6, _7_, 8   _2_, 3, 4   _4_, 5, 6

3, 6, _7_   _5_, 6, 7   _2_, 8, 9

_3_, 4, 5   6, 7, 8   5, _6_, 7

2, 3, _4_   1, 2, _3_   7, 8, _9_

2, _3_, 4   _1_, 2, 3   4, _5_, 6

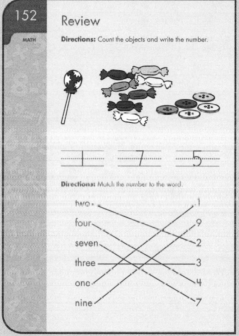

152 Review

MATH

Directions: Count the objects and write the number.

$\overline{1}$ $\overline{7}$ $\overline{5}$

Directions: Match the number to the word.

two 1
four 9
seven 2
three 3
one 4
nine 7

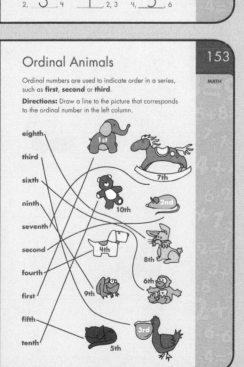

Ordinal Animals 153

MATH

Ordinal numbers are used to indicate order in a series, such as **first**, **second** or **third**.

Directions: Draw a line to the picture that corresponds to the ordinal number in the left column.

eighth
third
sixth
ninth
seventh
second
fourth
first
fifth
tenth

154 Get in Line!

MATH

Directions: These children are waiting to see a movie. Look at them and follow the directions.

MOVIES

1. Color the person who is **first** in line yellow.

2. Color the person who is **last** in line **brown**.

3. Color the person who is **second** in line pink.

4. Circle the person who is at the **end** of the line.

Add It Up: 1–2

Addition means "putting together" or adding two or more numbers to find the sum. "+" is a plus sign. It means to add the 2 numbers. "=" is an equals sign. It tells how much they are together.

Directions: Count the cats and tell how many.

$\begin{array}{r} +2 \\ \hline \end{array}$

Add It Up: 3–6

Directions: Practice writing the numbers and then add. Draw dots to help, if needed.

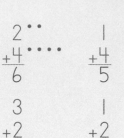

$\begin{array}{r} 2 \\ +4 \\ \hline 6 \end{array}$ $\begin{array}{r} 1 \\ +4 \\ \hline 5 \end{array}$

$\begin{array}{r} 3 \\ +2 \\ \hline 5 \end{array}$ $\begin{array}{r} 1 \\ +2 \\ \hline 3 \end{array}$

Add It Up: 6–8

Directions: Practice writing the numbers and then add. Draw dots to help, if needed.

$\begin{array}{r} 3 \\ +4 \\ \hline 7 \end{array}$ $\begin{array}{r} 5 \\ +1 \\ \hline 6 \end{array}$

$\begin{array}{r} 2 \\ +6 \\ \hline 8 \end{array}$ $\begin{array}{r} 4 \\ +4 \\ \hline 8 \end{array}$

Add It Up: 7–9

Directions: Practice writing the numbers and then add. Draw dots to help, if needed.

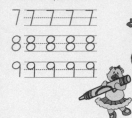

$\begin{array}{r} 8 \\ +1 \\ \hline 9 \end{array}$ $\begin{array}{r} 3 \\ +5 \\ \hline 8 \end{array}$

$\begin{array}{r} 2 \\ +7 \\ \hline 9 \end{array}$ $\begin{array}{r} 6 \\ +1 \\ \hline 7 \end{array}$

Add It Up!

Directions: Draw the correct number of dots next to the numbers in each problem. Add up the number of dots to find your answer.

Example:

$\begin{array}{r} 3 \\ +2 \\ \hline 5 \end{array}$ $2 + 2 = \underline{4}$

$\begin{array}{r} 4 \\ +2 \\ \hline 6 \end{array}$ $1 + 5 = \underline{6}$

$\begin{array}{r} 3 \\ +1 \\ \hline 4 \end{array}$ $4 + 3 = \underline{7}$

$\begin{array}{r} 6 \\ +2 \\ \hline 8 \end{array}$ $5 + 3 = \underline{8}$

Tool Time

Directions: Count the tools in each tool box. Write your answers in the blanks. Circle the problem that matches your answer.

4

$\left(\begin{array}{r} 2 \\ +2 \end{array}\right)$ $\begin{array}{r} 2 \\ +1 \end{array}$

6

$\begin{array}{r} 5 \\ +0 \end{array}$ $\left(\begin{array}{r} 4 \\ +2 \end{array}\right)$

8

$\left(\begin{array}{r} 6 \\ +2 \end{array}\right)$ $\begin{array}{r} 4 \\ +3 \end{array}$

5

$\begin{array}{r} 3 \\ +1 \end{array}$ $\left(\begin{array}{r} 2 \\ +3 \end{array}\right)$

In the Doghouse

161

MATH

Directions: Add the numbers. Put your answers in the doghouses.

Example: 4 + 2 = 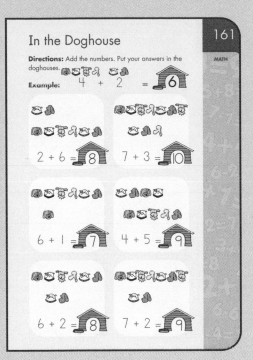 6

2 + 6 = 8

7 + 3 = 10

6 + 1 = 7

4 + 5 = 9

6 + 2 = 8

7 + 2 = 9

162

MATH

Subtraction Action: 1–3

Subtraction means "taking away" or subtracting one number from another. "−" is a minus sign. It means to subtract the second number from the first.

Directions: Practice writing the numbers and then subtract. Draw dots and cross them out, if needed.

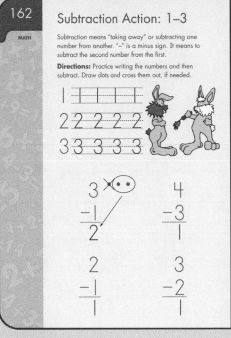

1

2 2 2 2 2

3 3 3 3 3

$$\begin{array}{r} 3 \\ -1 \\ \hline 2 \end{array}$$

$$\begin{array}{r} 4 \\ -3 \\ \hline 1 \end{array}$$

$$\begin{array}{r} 2 \\ -1 \\ \hline 1 \end{array}$$

$$\begin{array}{r} 3 \\ -2 \\ \hline 1 \end{array}$$

Subtraction Action: 3–6

163

MATH

Directions: Practice writing the numbers and then subtract. Draw dots and cross them out, if needed.

3 3 3 3 3

4 4 4 4 4

5 5 5 5 5

6 6 6 6 6

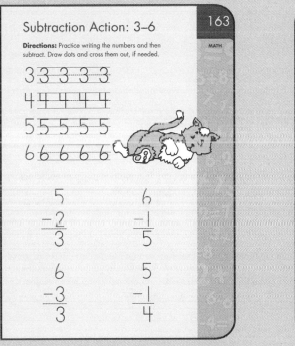

$$\begin{array}{r} 5 \\ -2 \\ \hline 3 \end{array}$$

$$\begin{array}{r} 6 \\ -1 \\ \hline 5 \end{array}$$

$$\begin{array}{r} 6 \\ -3 \\ \hline 3 \end{array}$$

$$\begin{array}{r} 5 \\ -1 \\ \hline 4 \end{array}$$

164

MATH

Fresh and Fruity

Directions: Count the fruit in each bowl. Write your answers in the blanks. Circle the problem that matches your answer.

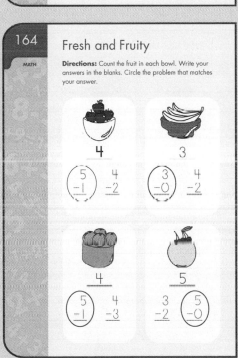

4

$$\begin{array}{r} 5 \\ -1 \end{array}$$ (circled) $$\begin{array}{r} 4 \\ -2 \end{array}$$

3

$$\begin{array}{r} 3 \\ -0 \end{array}$$ (circled) $$\begin{array}{r} 4 \\ -2 \end{array}$$

4

$$\begin{array}{r} 5 \\ -1 \end{array}$$ (circled) $$\begin{array}{r} 4 \\ -3 \end{array}$$

5

$$\begin{array}{r} 3 \\ -2 \end{array}$$ $$\begin{array}{r} 5 \\ -0 \end{array}$$ (circled)

Flower Power

165

MATH

Directions: Count the flowers. Write your answers in the blanks. Circle the problem that matches your answer.

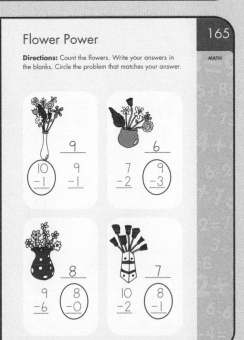

9

$$\begin{array}{r} 10 \\ -1 \end{array}$$ $$\begin{array}{r} 9 \\ -1 \end{array}$$

6

$$\begin{array}{r} 7 \\ -2 \end{array}$$ $$\begin{array}{r} 9 \\ -3 \end{array}$$ (circled)

8

$$\begin{array}{r} 9 \\ -6 \end{array}$$ $$\begin{array}{r} 8 \\ -0 \end{array}$$ (circled)

7

$$\begin{array}{r} 10 \\ -2 \end{array}$$ $$\begin{array}{r} 8 \\ -1 \end{array}$$ (circled)

166

MATH

Solve It!

Directions: Solve the problems. Remember, addition means "putting together" or adding two or more numbers to find the sum. Subtraction means "taking away" or subtracting one number from another.

1 + 3 = 4   4 − 3 = 1   4 + 5 = 9

6 + 1 = 7   7 − 2 = 5   8 − 4 = 4

9 − 1 = 8   10 − 3 = 7

5 − 2 = 3   6 + 3 = 9

8 + 2 = 10   5 + 5 = 10

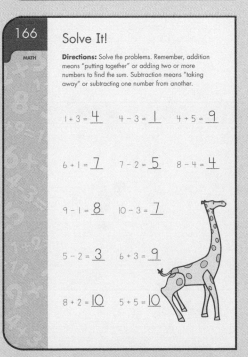

Patchwork Math 167

MATH

Remember, addition means "putting together" or adding two or more numbers to find the sum. Subtraction means "taking away" or subtracting one number from another.

Directions: Solve the problems. From your answers, use the code to color the quilt.

Color:

6's blue

7's yellow

8's green

9's red

10's orange

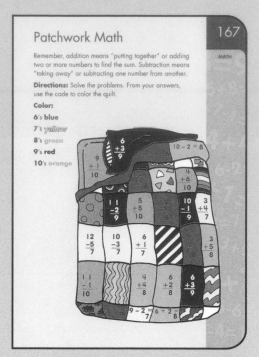

168 Review

MATH

Directions: Trace the numbers. Work the problems

1 2 3 4 5 6 7 8 9 10

$$\begin{array}{r} 9 \\ -3 \\ \hline 6 \end{array} \qquad \begin{array}{r} 6 \\ +2 \\ \hline 8 \end{array} \qquad \begin{array}{r} 3 \\ +4 \\ \hline 7 \end{array}$$

$$\begin{array}{r} 5 \\ +4 \\ \hline 9 \end{array} \qquad \begin{array}{r} 9 \\ -5 \\ \hline 4 \end{array} \qquad \begin{array}{r} 7 \\ +2 \\ \hline 9 \end{array}$$

$$\begin{array}{r} 4 \\ -2 \\ \hline 2 \end{array} \qquad \begin{array}{r} 6 \\ +3 \\ \hline 9 \end{array} \qquad \begin{array}{r} 9 \\ -7 \\ \hline 2 \end{array}$$

Get to Know Zero 169

MATH

Directions: Write the number.

Example:

How many monkeys? 3

How many monkeys? 0

How many kites? 3

How many kites? 0

How many flowers? 2

How many flowers? 0

How many apples? 4

How many apples? 0

170 Picture This: Addition

MATH

Directions: Solve the number problem under each picture.

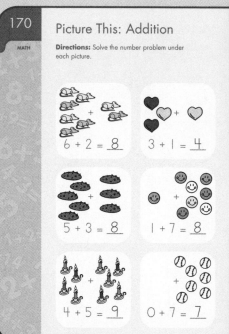

6 + 2 = 8   3 + 1 = 4

5 + 3 = 8   1 + 7 = 8

4 + 5 = 9   0 + 7 = 7

Picture This: Addition 171

MATH

Directions: Solve the number problem under each picture.

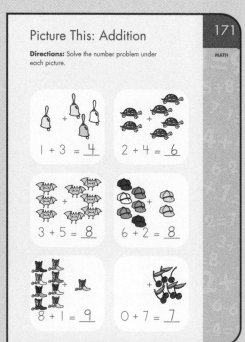

1 + 3 = 4   2 + 4 = 6

3 + 5 = 8   6 + 2 = 8

8 + 1 = 9   0 + 7 = 7

172 Picture This: Subtraction

MATH

Directions: Solve the number problem under each picture.

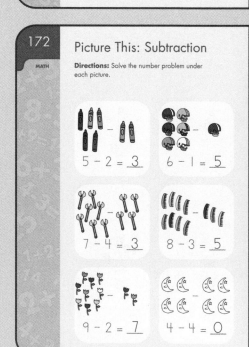

5 - 2 = 3   6 - 1 = 5

7 - 4 = 3   8 - 3 = 5

9 - 2 = 7   4 - 4 = 0

Picture This: Subtraction
173
MATH

Directions: Solve the number problem under each picture.

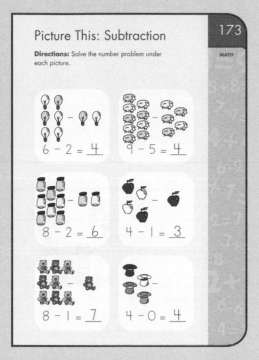

6 − 2 = 4

9 − 5 = 4

8 − 2 = 6

4 − 1 = 3

8 − 1 = 7

4 − 0 = 4

174
MATH

Know Your Place

The place value of a digit, or numeral, is shown by where it is in the number. For example, in the number **23**, **2** has the place value of **tens**, and **3** is **ones**.

Directions: Count the groups of ten crayons and write the number by the word **tens**. Count the other crayons and write the number by the word **ones**.

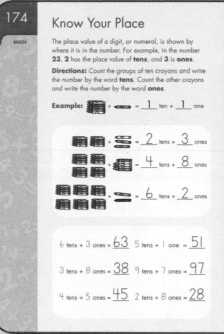

Example: = 1 ten + 1 one

= 2 tens + 3 ones

= 4 tens + 8 ones

= 6 tens + 2 ones

6 tens + 3 ones = 63   5 tens + 1 one = 51

3 tens + 8 ones = 38   9 tens + 7 ones = 97

4 tens + 5 ones = 45   2 tens + 8 ones = 28

Know Your Place
175
MATH

Directions: Write the answers in the correct spaces.

	tens	ones	
3 tens, 2 ones	3	2	= 32
3 tens, 7 ones	3	7	= 37
9 tens, 1 one	9	1	= 91
5 tens, 6 ones	5	6	= 56
6 tens, 5 ones	6	5	= 65
6 tens, 8 ones	6	8	= 68
2 tens, 8 ones	2	8	= 28
4 tens, 9 ones	4	9	= 49
1 ten, 4 ones	1	4	= 14
8 tens, 2 ones	8	2	= 82
4 tens, 2 ones	4	2	= 42

28 = 2 tens, 8 ones
64 = 6 tens, 4 ones
56 = 5 tens, 6 ones
72 = 7 tens, 2 ones
38 = 3 tens, 8 ones
17 = 1 ten, 7 ones
63 = 6 tens, 3 ones
12 = 1 ten, 2 ones

176
MATH

On a Ride with Five

Directions: Count by fives to draw a path to the playground.

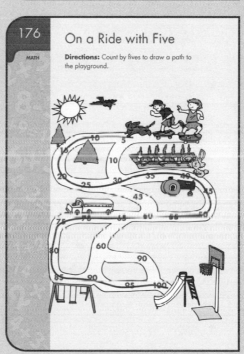

On the Trail of Tens
177
MATH

Directions: Count in order by tens to draw the path the boy takes to the store.

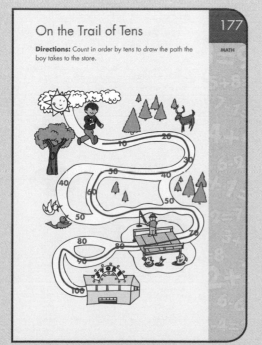

178
MATH

Counting on Crayons

Directions: Circle groups of ten crayons. Add the remaining ones to make the correct number.

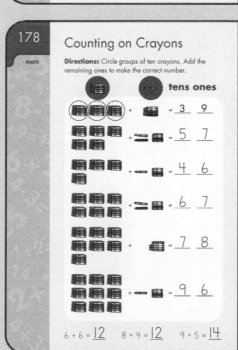

	tens	ones
	3	9
	5	7
	4	6
	6	7
	7	8
	9	6

6 + 6 = 12   8 + 4 = 12   9 + 5 = 14

Crayon Cross-out

Directions: Count the crayons in each group. Put an **X** through the number of crayons being subtracted. How many are left?

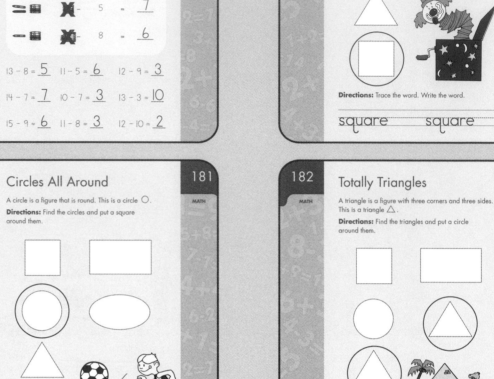

- 5 - <u>10</u>
- 4 - <u>7</u>
- 7 - <u>6</u>
- 6 - <u>8</u>
- 5 - <u>7</u>
- 8 - <u>6</u>

$13 - 8 = \underline{5}$ $11 - 5 = \underline{6}$ $12 - 9 = \underline{3}$

$14 - 7 = \underline{7}$ $10 - 7 = \underline{3}$ $13 - 3 = \underline{10}$

$15 - 9 = \underline{6}$ $11 - 8 = \underline{3}$ $12 - 10 = \underline{2}$

Fair and Square

A square is a figure with four corners and four sides of the same length. This is a square □.

Directions: Find the squares and circle them.

Directions: Trace the word. Write the word.

square   square

Circles All Around

A circle is a figure that is round. This is a circle ○.

Directions: Find the circles and put a square around them.

Directions: Trace the word. Write the word.

circle   circle

Totally Triangles

A triangle is a figure with three corners and three sides. This is a triangle △.

Directions: Find the triangles and put a circle around them.

Directions: Trace the word. Write the word.

triangle   triangle

Make Room for Rectangles

A rectangle is a figure four corners and four sides. Sides opposite each other are the same length. This is a rectangle □.

Directions: Find the rectangles and put a circle around them.

Directions: Trace the word. Write the word.

rectangle   rectangle

Ovals and Diamonds

An oval is an egg-shaped figure. A diamond is a figure with four sides of the same length. It's corners form points at the top, sides and bottom. This is an oval ○. This is a diamond ◇.

Directions: Color the ovals **red**. Color the diamonds **blue**.

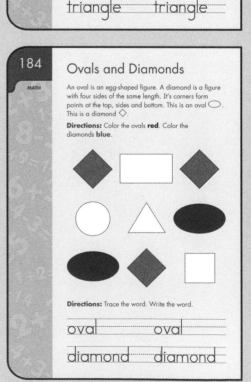

Directions: Trace the word. Write the word.

oval   oval

diamond   diamond

Review

Review

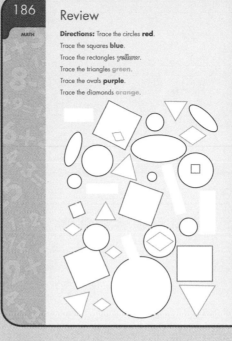

Shape Up

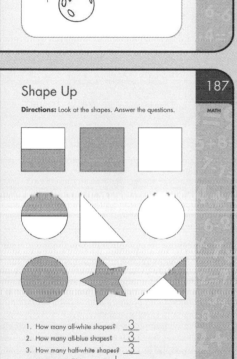

1. How many all-white shapes? 3
2. How many all-blue shapes? 3
3. How many half-white shapes? 3
4. How many all-blue stars? 1
5. How many all-white circles? 1
6. How many half-blue shapes? 3

Ship Shape

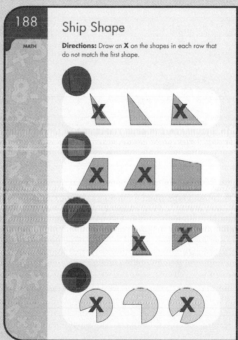

Pattern Play

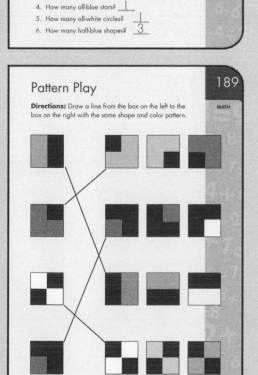

Pattern Play

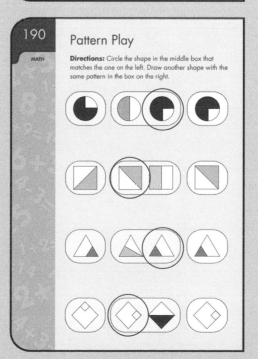

Pattern Play

191

MATH

Directions: Fill in the missing shape in each row. Then, color it.

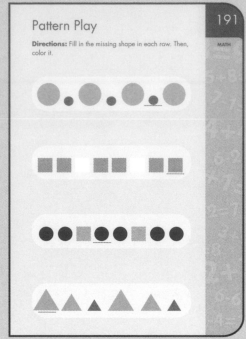

192

MATH

Fraction Action: Whole and Half

A fraction is a number that names part of a whole, such as $\frac{1}{2}$ or $\frac{3}{4}$.

Directions: Color half of each object.

Example:

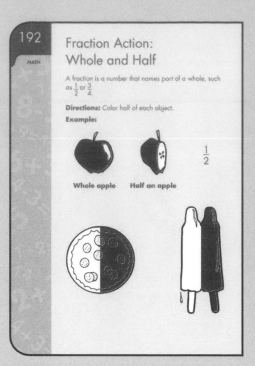

Whole apple   Half an apple $\frac{1}{2}$

Fraction Action: Halves $\frac{1}{2}$

193

MATH

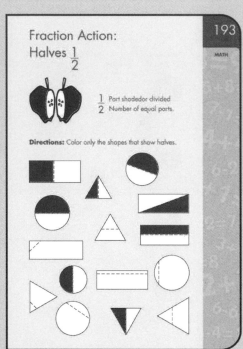

$\frac{1}{2}$ Part shaded or divided
        Number of equal parts.

Directions: Color only the shapes that show halves.

194

MATH

Fraction Action: Thirds and Fourths

Directions: Each object has 3 equal parts. Color one section.

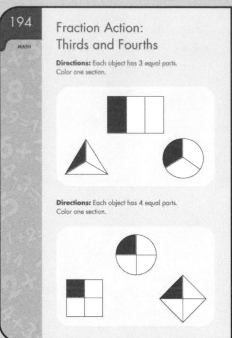

Directions: Each object has 4 equal parts. Color one section.

Review

195

MATH

Directions: Count the equal parts, then write the fraction.

Example:

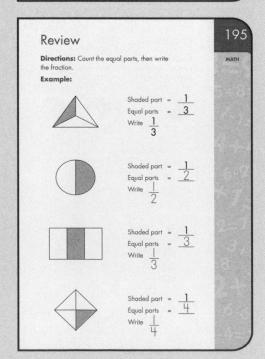

Shaded part = $\frac{1}{3}$
Equal parts = $\frac{1}{3}$
Write $\frac{1}{3}$

Shaded part = $\frac{1}{2}$
Equal parts = $\frac{1}{2}$
Write $\frac{1}{2}$

Shaded part = $\frac{1}{3}$
Equal parts = $\frac{1}{3}$
Write $\frac{1}{3}$

Shaded part = $\frac{1}{4}$
Equal parts = $\frac{1}{4}$
Write $\frac{1}{4}$

196

MATH

On the Right Track

Directions: Draw a straight line from A to B. Use a different color crayon for each line.

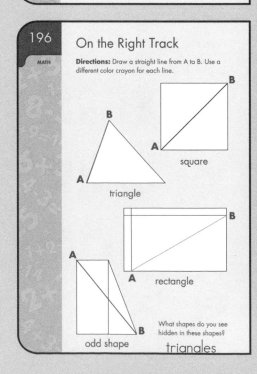

square

triangle

rectangle

odd shape

What shapes do you see hidden in these shapes?

triangles

Finding a Friend | 197 | MATH

Help Megan find Mark.

Directions: Trace a path from Megan to Mark.

Paths may vary

How many different paths
can she follow to reach him? __8__

198 | MATH | On the Honey Trail

Directions: Use different colors to trace three paths the
bear could take to get the honey.

Right on Time! | 199 | MATH

The short hand of the clock tells the hour. The long hand
tells how many minutes after the hour. When the minute
hand is on the **12**, it is the beginning of the hour.

Directions: Look at each clock. Write the time.

Example:

__3__ o'clock

__9__ o'clock   __1__ o'clock

__8__ o'clock   __6__ o'clock

__2__ o'clock   __10__ o'clock

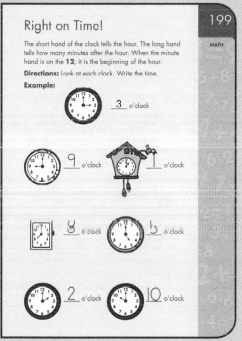

200 | MATH | It's About Time

The short hand of the clock tells the hour. The long hand
tells how many minutes after the hour. When the minute
hand is on the **6**, it is on the half-hour. A half-hour is
thirty minutes. It is written **:30**, such as **5:30**.

Directions: Look at each clock. Write the time.

Example:

hour half-hour
__1__ : __30__

__5__ : __30__   __6__ : __30__

__4__ : __30__   __7__ : __30__

__2__ : __30__   __10__ : __30__

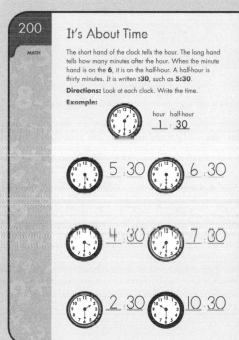

Rock Around the Clock | 201 | MATH

Directions: Fill in the numbers on the clock face. Count
by fives around the clock.

There are 60 minutes in one hour.

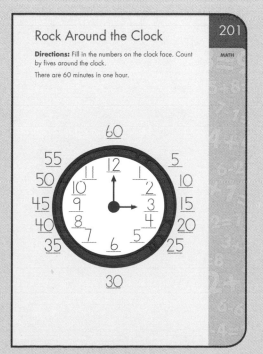

202 | MATH | Time to Match

Directions: Match the time on the clock with
the digital time.

10:00

5:00

3:00

9:00

2:00

Review

Directions: Look at the time on the digital clocks and draw the hands on the clocks.

203

MATH

10:00   5:00

Directions: Look at each clock. Write the time.

3 o'clock   2 o'clock

Directions: Look at each clock. Write the time.

1:30   10:30   4:30

204

MATH

Money Sense

A penny is worth one cent. It is written **1¢** or **$.01**. A nickel is worth five cents. It is written **5¢** or **$.05**. A dime is worth ten cents. It is written **10¢** or **$.10**.

Directions: Add the coins pictured and write the total amounts in the blanks.

Example:

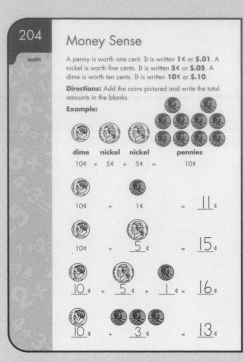

dime   nickel   nickel   pennies

10¢ = 5¢ + 5¢ =   10¢

10¢ + 1¢   = 11¢

10¢ + 5 ¢   = 15¢

10¢ + 5 ¢ + 1 ¢ = 16¢

10¢ + 3 ¢   = 13¢

How Much?

Directions: Match the amounts in each purse to the price tags.

205

MATH

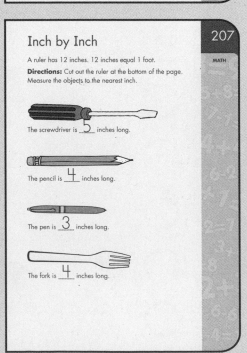

7¢

12¢

3¢

18¢

206

MATH

Review

Directions: What time is it?

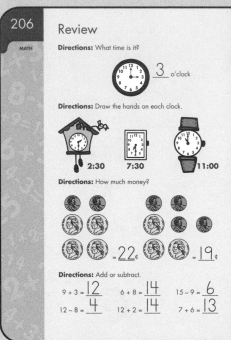

3 o'clock

Directions: Draw the hands on each clock.

2:30   7:30   11:00

Directions: How much money?

22¢   19¢

Directions: Add or subtract.

9 + 3 = 12   6 + 8 = 14   15 – 9 = 6
12 – 8 = 4   12 + 2 = 14   7 + 6 = 13

Inch by Inch

A ruler has 12 inches. 12 inches equal 1 foot.

Directions: Cut out the ruler at the bottom of the page. Measure the objects to the nearest inch.

207

MATH

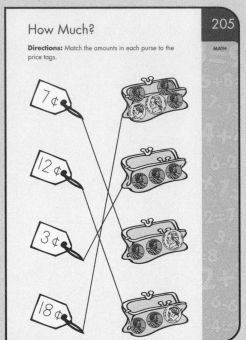

The screwdriver is 5 inches long.

The pencil is 4 inches long.

The pen is 3 inches long.

The fork is 4 inches long.

41	42	43	44	45	46	47	48	49	50
51	52	53	54	55	56	57	58	59	60
61	62	63	64	65	66	67	68	69	70
71	72	73	74	75	76	77	78	79	80
81	82	83	84	85	86	87	88	89	90
91	92	93	94	95	96	97	98	99	100

Numbers 1-100 Chart

1	2	3	4	5	6	7	8	9	10
11	12	13	14	15	16	17	18	19	20
21	22	23	24	25	26	27	28	29	30
31	32	33	34	35	36	37	38	39	40